Advance

Token to
Boardwalk

28 New Jersey Poets

Introduction by Joel Oppenheimer

Poets & Writers of New Jersey

This anthology represents a collective effort by all poets included. Special services were performed by Toi Derricotte, Penny Bihler, Lois Van Houten, Alice Kolb, Shaun Farragher, Dan Georgakas, Rod Tulloss, Tom Weatherly, David Keller, Mary King.

The following presses have contributed to the production of this book: Buffalo Gnats Press, From Here Press, Hudson River Press, Smyrna Press, USl Poets' Cooperative.

We acknowledge the following magazines and anthologies in which many of the poems of *Advance Token to Boardwalk* first appeared: *Albatross, American Poetry Review, Aspen Writers Conference Chapbook, Bergen Poets 1, Berkeley Poets Cooperative, Black Box, Brooklyn Ferry, Campfires of the Resistance, Center, Challenge, Community of Friends, Confrontation, Dacotah Territory, The Denver Quarterly,* From Here Press, *Gilt Edge, Gravida, Greenfield Review, Haiku Magazine, Hearse, Hiram Poetry Journal, Ironwood, Journal of New Jersey Poets, The Literary Tabloid, Minnesota Review, Montclair State Quarterly, Paterson Anthology, Paterson Pieces, Poetry Northwest, Poetry Roundtable, Route 80, So This is the Light, Statesman, The Stone, Stone Country, Street Cries, Third Thing, Three Red Stars, Tightrope, US1 Worksheets, Write Poems Women: An Anthology.*

Also acknowledged:

Stephen Dunn, *Full of Lust and Good Usage*, Carnegie-Mellon University Press, 1976.

Dan Georgakas, *And All Living Things Their Children*, Bb Books, 1969 and Shameless Hussy, 1972.

Alicia Ostriker, *Songs*, Holt, Rinehart & Winston, 1969.

Rod Tulloss, *December 1975*, From Here Press, 1977.

Lois Van Houten, *Behind the Door*, Stone Country Press, 1976.

ISBN: 0-918266-06-8

Typesetting by Bill & May Robinson, Box 1296, Benson, AZ 85602.

Book design by Rod Tulloss.

Printed in the United States of America.

Contents

Introduction

Once upon a time there was a big city, a metropolis, where everything was alive and filled with energy, and when you went away from that place, you were nowhere. At least that's the way the legend went, whether it was true or not. Manhattan was where you went from places like Kansas as well as from towns like Yonkers, right next door. And if you were from New Jersey and you came, you lied, because everyone in Manhattan knew New Jersey was the end of the world, even if it was right across the river. It was a place of factories and fumes at one end, and the boonies at the other, with a couple of slums in between. There were no poems there is what we all were certain of.

We knew William Carlos Williams had lived and worked and wrote his life out there, but I suppose we figured he was such a genius he could get poems from anywhere; maybe, that he'd picked Jersey as his own little hell to wrest the soul from.

But there were people who believed in their place, who learned from what the good gray doctor had done, and from others like Allen Ginsburg, coming out of those awful cities, and who believed there were poems there, and wrote them.

All of which will serve as my apology, if not to New Jersey, then to these poets, here, in this anthology. Not all of them are Jersey-born, but they all damned well have committed themselves to it, as well as to their work, and the fruit of their commitment is here, in these pages.

I've met some of them, known some of them as friends first, others as students and then friends, and I suppose that's one reason they offered me the privilege of putting these few words at the beginning of their anthology, to serve as introduction, as if a collection of live, living poetry needed one.

But I understand the need to ask for some words first—it's in the hope that someone, somewhere, will stop, pay attention, read the poems. That seems to be a very hard thing to do in this country, its been discussed over and over and won't be here. What interests me far more than the fact that most Americans distrust the act of poetry is the fact that there have always been, always are, Americans who insist on writing it, who insist on using their quite considerable skills to pursue the hopeless task of getting their perceptions of their place down on paper for their countrymen to see.

So we have *Advance Token to Boardwalk*, the name itself taken from that one magical place in the whole state, Atlantic City—at least the one magical place known by us outlanders. And from the most famous game made in our time, the indestructible Monopoly, killer of endless rainy hours across the world. Well, why not? Why not a game? Games and poetry are in the end the only things we stretch ourselves with, no matter how we try to cut ourselves to other philosophies. The strange limited world of a game within its rules, destroying 'real' time and space; the strange *un*-limited world of poetry equally destructive of the 'real,' only to make it even more real, to make our lives more real.

The poem serves, always, as the strong underbeat of where we are, both literally, as in New Jersey, and figuratively, as in our souls and self. I am impressed here by the number of women, and the strength of their poems, the anger, the irony, the love—and impressed as much by how the men respond to this new world we live in always. Quieter, it is almost as if, finally, they are listening, after all those centuries of shouting. From this role reversal, if it be such, only good can come, because if each is truly learning new ways to perceive, then all are gaining.

But I don't want this to sound like a sociological tract. What counts are the poems:

> Relax. This won't last long.
> Or if it does, or if the lines
> make you sleepy or bored,
> give in to sleep, turn on
> the T.V., deal the cards.
> This poem is built to withstand
> such things. Its feelings
> cannot be hurt. . . .

as Stephen Dunn tells us in his ''Poem for People Who Are Understandably Too Busy to Read Poetry.'' Toi Derricotte warns us:

> buried birds
> are usually
> dead.
> fallen from the sky
> because of too much
> something.
>   too much high.
>   too much steep.
>   too much long.
>   too much deep.
> but sometimes
> one has been known
> to go underground. . . .

in ''unburying the bird.'' Perhaps that is what is happening in this anthology: the bird is being unburied, brought out into the open, the harsh glare of New Jersey's reality. It would be futile, and foolish too, to go through the work picking a phrase here and there, an image, a perception, for you. I want you to do that, and so I'll not pick poet by poet, telling you those I love and those I like, and those you ought to listen to and get angry, and those you ought to smile with. That's your work—and your pleasure.

What I will do is beg you to do that work. It's important for you as much as for the poets. After all, all this anthology really took from them was time and money and care and dedication, and time and money can be made somehow, and care and dedication will continue to be given whether you listen or not.

But it's important that you listen. It seems to me that among the many breakdowns apparent in our rush bigness and the better life, one that's gone unnoticed but that looms so large is the return to the local—and to the locale, if you will. Poets are learning they must speak to their 'community,' to those involved in the same things they are. If they speak well and truly their voices and their poems will be heard by others, outside the community, but they must start within.

That's the most important thing about this book, and the most impressive. These poets are speaking to all of us, yes, but first they are speaking to their neighbors, not in a parochial sense, but in the age-old way of the real singer: to take those things held in common and make them uncommon, so that all may become more. Williams says in *Paterson:* No ideas but in things, and speaks of a local pride. These two touchstones always have been the root of the poem and of life itself, but for centuries we have moved away from them, and now we pay for it.

Listen to your poets, they sing of you and to you, while they like Whitman sing of themselves. Our selves are all we have, and thus what we have best to give to others. And in that giving the singing rings loud and clear to tell us all what we are, can be, or have become.

I thank these poets for this book, and congratulate them on it, and wait for more.

joel oppenheimer
august 1977

Stephen Dunn

THE MAN WHO NEVER LOSES HIS BALANCE

He walks the high wire in his sleep.
The tent is blue, it is perpetual
afternoon. He is walking between
the open legs of his mother
and the grave. Always. The audience knows this
is out of their hands. The audience
is fathers whose kites are lost, children
who want to be terrified into joy.
He is so high above them, so capable
(with a single, calculated move)
of making them care for him
that he's sick of the risks
he never really takes.
The tent is blue. Outside is a world
that is blue. Inside him
a blueness that could crack
like china if he ever hit bottom.
Every performance, deep down,
he tries one real plunge
off to the side, where the net ends.
But it never ends.

A FEW NIGHTS AND DAYS

He foresaw a lagoon
cut off from its larger body,
capillaries floating like plankton
in a cadaver, a man with his arms
joyously around men and women. . .

When he woke it was a Tuesday,
the porchlight still on
and umbrage in the air
over breakfast; the woman he loved
had her eyes closed
looking for holes in his arguments.
He muffed his mouth, hating her,
wondering if she knew she'd be dead
in thirty or forty years,
hating himself and the stone wall
he could build in seconds
around his heart, hating the nationtalk,
the journalism between people
who simply want to touch.

His daughter came in with the
alphabet in her mouth;
how, out of love, he squeezed her
until she was breathless—
how, if she were Vietnamese
and on the run, beyond hunger,
scabbed, whimpering,
he might, out of love, squeeze her
until she was dead.
And then it was Wednesday and Thursday
and every morning the porchlight
a dull beacon in the sun.

***

He dreamed the last suck
of a falling star, that intake
of air before one begins
to dazzle the world—
and the regular breath
of people everywhere
contemplating insurance. . .

2

And he found himself
on the edge of nothing
in particular, in the middle
of a bed big enough for three victims
of the six-o'clock news.
He made love to his wife
whispering *this is how you steal*
moments from the end of your life
and they knocked the clock off the nighttable
the covers onto the floor
and the orphans
took their big eyes elsewhere.

But only for a while.
The 20th century was relentless—
there were satellites near the moon
reporting everything,
children wanting to know
why squirrels didn't look both ways
before cars hit them,
the ordinary desolation
of handshakes and lunches.
Not even sex or his natural capacity
for self-deception did much good
anymore.

On the last day of the week
in a year in a lifetime of last days
he left his house
daydreaming his shadow
had shed its dark clothes.
The streets were crowded.
He saw the flesh of beautiful women—
all flesh—as flesh that is dying,
but he said to himself *every touch*
is a renewal, every touch is
a renewal

and he touched no one.

POEM FOR PEOPLE WHO ARE UNDERSTANDABLY
TOO BUSY TO READ POETRY

Relax. This won't last long.
Or if it does, or if the lines
make you sleepy or bored,
give in to sleep, turn on
the T.V., deal the cards.
This poem is built to withstand
such things. Its feelings
cannot be hurt.
They exist somewhere in the poet,
and I am far away.
Pick it up any time. Start it
in the middle if you wish.
It is as approachable as melodrama,
and can offer you violence
if it is violence you like.
Look, *there's a man on a sidewalk.*
In a red puddle, I spot my dreams
beside his open head.
They've never been clearer.
This is your poem
and I know you're busy at the office
or the kids are into your last good nerve.
Maybe it's sex you've always wanted.
Well, *they lie together*
like the party's unbuttoned coats,
slumped on the bed
waiting for drunken arms
to move them. There,
I don't think you want me to go on.
Everyone has his expectations, but this
is a poem for the entire family.
Right now, Budweiser
is dripping from a waterfall,
deodorants are hissing into armpits
of people you resemble,
and *the two lovers are dressing now,*
saying farewell.
I don't know what music this poem
can come up with, but clearly
it is needed. For it's apparent
they will never see each other again
and we need music for this
because there was never music when he or she
left *you* standing on that corner.

You see, I want this poem to be nicer
than life. I want you to look at it
when anxiety zigzags your stomach
and the last tranquilizer is gone
and you need someone to tell you
I'll be here when you want me
like the sound inside a shell.
The poem is saying that to you now.
But do not give up anything for this poem.
It doesn't expect much. It will never say more
than listening can explain.
Just keep it in your attache case
or in your house. And if you are not asleep
by now, or bored beyond sense,
the poem wants you to laugh. Laugh at
yourself, laugh at this poem, at all poetry.
Come on:

Good. Now here's what poetry can do.
Imagine yourself a caterpillar.
There's an awful shrug and, suddenly,
you're beautiful for as long as you live.

TRUCK STOP: MINNESOTA

The waitress looks at my face
as if it were a small tip.
I'm tempted to come back at her
with *java*
but I say *coffee,* politely,
and tell her how I want it.
Her body has the alert sleepiness
of a cat's. Her face
the indecency of a billboard.
She is the America I would like to love.
Sweetheart, the truckers call her.
Honey. Doll.
For each of them, she smiles.
I envy them,
I'm full of lust and good usage,
lost here.
I imagine every man she's left with
has smelled of familiar food,
has peppered her with wild slang
until she was damp and loose.
I do nothing but ask for a check
and drift out into the night air—
let my dreams lift
her tired feet off the ground
into the sweet, inarticulate
democracy beyond my ears—
and keep moving until I'm home
in the middle of my country.

Madeline T. Bass

PROLOGUE

the life in my house
is beyond me
every time I sleep
some   thing
stirs
downstairs

          taller
than wind in
the locust tree
the chimney
the oldest son

something wild

tonight
in the attic
just above my bed
a squirrel scratches (call it that
in hope against rat, snake,
skunk) not much louder than
dessications of red maple

but less
mystery and belligerence
than in what is
reclining
by my fire
inside the flat body
of a man I knew once

I HAD NO SISTER

[*I have a little sister
and she lives in the country
and her name is Barbara Jane,
I have a little sister
and she lives in the city
and her name is Barbara Jane.*]

—nursery rhyme sung by
Mady Tiger in 1936

*this poem is dedicated to
Barbara Jane Tiger Rubens,
b. 1937*

for a long time
I didn't have a sister
and my feet fit
inside the hexagons
on the sidewalks
of Central Park West
so no bears bit

for a long time
I crossed alone
then I gave her a name:
it was Barbara Jane

she turned out braided
big and blue
with a guitar and bright bonnets
and she favored you

she followed me everywhere
I never allowed her
she played house with me
but she wasn't the baby

she was afraid of me
so I beat her up
I climbed trees faster
and she forgave me
she begged me to let her
under the table

she lived in the block room
and when she took baths
Mother dried her with lovesongs
the longest lullabyes
gold rings and nut trees
"and Babsy's a drummer
          who drums for the king. . ."

she had luminous eyes
and when I was 39
Mrs. Sokoloff said
my daughter was beautiful,
she said, "Does she look like your sister?
I hear she's the beauty."

No.

I had no sister.
I pushed her
into a hexagon,
pram and all,
by the comfort station
gone and good riddance!
I had no sister
a little fat tidbit
in a pink bunting
was eaten by zoo lions

I had no sister
I wrapped a dydee
in Mother's gold shawl
and rolled a doughball
under the table
I stuffed something
fleshy and peaceful
into the maple crotch

I pushed a shadow
between the hedgerows
I dropped a redness
out of the top of the apple tree
I flushed the toilet
no, no, no, not me
I had no sister

I had a blue velvet dress
with white buttons
I had patent leather mary janes
I had stiff brown leggings
shaped like jodhpurs
for handing down
to cousin Mary Ellen
I had an Aunt Sadie
across from the Planetarium
who made coddled eggs
and willed me
her dining room table
I had a Charlie McCarthy
and a cocker-poodle
a sidewalk for hopscotch
a best friend
who knew most of my secrets
a big brick house
and metal curlers
a "couple" upstairs
a garage with a top floor
and two parents somewhere:
a mother in white and an old bald father.
I had no sister.

Then I invent her.
She lives in the city.
She lives in California
She's bigger than California.
I can call her in the morning.
I can call her at night.
She has long brown hair,
a color TV, big breasts,
and lots of problems.
She doesn't hide under the table much,
she laughs very loud,
she plays the zither, she teaches everyone
how to sing.
She can walk
even when her toes are broken,
that's how much of a grown-up she is.
So I'm going to travel
across the country
to see her soon.
It's no mystery to have
a sister who answers
the names I call her.

10/74

THE INTRUDER

a stranger in my house
stalks books.
he is loose
across my carpets, long
and tangled
on old hangers,
wipes out my nightmares.
like a spider, creeps
in pots. like boys, pees
suddenly in my private toilet.
never announces
the slicing of an apple
or the recline of upholstered armchairs.
my radio is drifting.
one morning all the alarm clocks
were broken. the one
familiar with hidden summerwear
keeps
eating crackers.
my kitchen crumbles, but
if I retreat upstairs
a black fly buzzes there, growing
enormous. I never buy cheeses
or dresses, and I try to slice roasts thin,
quickly, to outwit him through dinner,
despite stains on stairs,
broken hairs in the brushes,
foul piles of shells
in our garbage. the sentinels
I used to hire
have gone south where work is outdoors
and more honest. hulking shadows
block my windows.
my curtains stick shut
like the rusty firescreen,
embers blink and throw dust.

a scratchy noise: are the walls
chalking? one or two footsteps
at unexpected hours: 2:00 after lunch
or 9:00 in my evening. I hide in bed
and fear the finger. I hear
pomegranates open to seeds.
I'm hopeless against
the red drip. I dream
of milkweed witches
that won't float off
and autumn pods popping marigold. I
dream that I am waking up
                and all the evergreens we planted
have been uprooted.
even the spreading holly. my nude house
cringes. my children stand gasping
in a lack of question.

he curls his hand around my bladder
like a bear.
suddenly —he is changing— his skin
shines, he flicks his green tongue
on my neck, my garden burns
to orange. to russet. to brown.
by rote I collect the dead
zinnias, the spindled chrysanthemums.

now he chortles.
now he wrinkles today's papers.
now he builds a fine fire.
now he relaxes with a cocktail.
I hear the sparks.
I hear the ice cubes.

now I will look at his
ancient face.

I will throw
his ring in
the kindling.

Alice Kolb

A HYMN TO #8

Wait said Robert, almost serenely, you'll see
    She lay supine
    black hole in her gut
    decaying, flaking breast
    come to term.
    but not intact

Oh, no . . . Yes, said Robert. The desert was empty
in the pink-gold light of the setting sun. The
mirage was gone. A few dust devils whirled and
fell apart, way out on the horizon
    Her body stretched o
    o u t
    there
    within touch of
    sterile gloves, sterile surgeon

The man with no cap in the rain? Ah, him! snapped
the woman. Sick. We heard him go off coughing the
national anthem
    The woman
    gave
    out.
    sweet
    terrors

In the windows the sugar skulls with names on
their snowy brows. The faces of the father, the
mother, the daughter, the son, were glowing now,
looking off at the desert
    The ceiling
    became
    glazed
    blue
    porcelain

Robert let out a huge groan of bereavement.

THE STAIRS

The stairs sang ever higher
in wavering snatches of Spring

wheat fields
trains without tracks
tracks without trains

diddle-de-dum diddle-de-dum
the sum adding always
to black

heal marks
on window sills

reflections of chalk drawings
just beyond

the short walk
through the glass window panes

SOMEWHERE NORTH OF DETROIT
wind is turning birch leaves
in the sun

wind is sifting through the heap
of a woman

sitting with rump firm on wood
binoculars in hand   bird watching
feeding her eyes with flashes of red

who hears her cry
as grass pleats her ankles
to the bench

Gingerbread lady
sparrows are picking at the icing
on your dress

a cardinal is carrying away
your cinnamon button eyes

DON'T WAKE UP TO THE WORMS
that are crawling on your mind
always. You never learned to
live with them

as walking in Procession
afraid to throw out
the rose petals
avoiding the soft depths

like taking a shotgun one day
to blow red shapes
through your mouth
onto the ceiling

ON THE LAST MORNING OF SUMMER

STREETLIGHT SHINING THROUGH THE BACK:

Past tubes and empty breathings a light
to comfort to heal perhaps
a small patch of sun
on the meadow of decay.
beneath her I feel twistings of the animal
who never has been to the land of
immovable pain before:

THE LEAPINGS TOWARD MY EYES:

teeth fully exposed. This Wild Thing's
broken back.
well. This Thing will be disposed of.
bring on the waters of baptism
a drowning of This Thing running
in tight circles of why and how
the spirit will renew itself in:

THE RUNNING OBLATION TO THE SAMENESS
OF THE NEED FOR:

moon. when will you look down to see these
oceans
holding the magnet to the idiot's hand
and who will tell will tell the cry to fade
to quiet spaces.
and who can damn the one who waits to leap
toward another light place where the wild
can wander outside that room of dangling tubes
and rows of eyes dimming:

ON AN OPENING DOOR THAT LEADS FINALLY OUT:

stepping forward that is all
I can see.
forward.
neither up or down
the black not only all around
it is and of in place of
what was left
inside.
this utter smashing into.

light

Jon Klimo

CAPE COD

We are both silent as I change her
And delicately tighten
The drawstring neck.
Wrapping my baby in a sack,
I sneak from the tent.

The sun will grow right out of the ocean
In less than an hour,
And I've got to show her,
Hold my daughter up to Nature.

In the chill earliness, there's a real fear:
The delicate tremble that we'll miss it,
And like the way they wouldn't let me
Be there for my baby's birth,
I'd find again all had arrived without me,
Let down sideways, hungry gulls
And human jetsam
In the kind of light you always wake to,
The drive back, the baby crying,
Sea and sky already parted
For that eye of fire,
Plain as day in the rearview mirror.

Arrowing through the turning point
Of full moon into morning light,
Thriving on seizures of cold water
Swelling in the cello body,
I drive pursued
With the prospect of losing
Personal touch with an abstract longing.

Stop sign, and I flip my arm
Over to hold her
From going forward,
Brake in the lot at the base of the dunes,
Grab one love and head for the other.

We sit together and it happens,
Ever so slowly, like a flower.
How strange to think that I've won
Something. But I have.
I've brought a glass blown from our flesh
And let it fill with ocean morning.

Little pawn in this serious game of thirst,
You too will grow to use this world,
Suffering the dislocated heart.
The homesickness goes on forever.

THE EYES OF THE BEHOLDER

In the surprising dark of London
At 4:00 in the afternoon, my daughter
And I go for our daily
Walk before supper
Down the hills of Islington.

Left over from the day, a few small fires
Smolder in the rubble at the edge of lots
Whose streets have names right out of The Tempest.

Heading off Prospero with her on my shoulders,
I pick my way, a little off balance,
Over bricks and into the smoke
And bombed quality of a demolition site

With 'Clear All Basements' and 'Row 19'
Painted over the universal
Cupid and cursing neighborhood algebra
Chalked on the walls of the condemned.

I shift to stay upwind
Of the biggest bonfire of them all.
What seem like chunks of cars, houses,
Trees, cling together, fighting for air
Through blankets of smoke
To bear a floodlight of tearing oranges.

The iconic ivory of the one dead man
I've ever seen returns to me
As I face a further row of houses,
Abandoned, cold,
Almost every window broken.

Sometimes a situation presents itself
As pure poetry, solid
As a medallion, but ghosting over
To a lens on a throat that's singing:
As if so much of the inanimate world
Was calling through its collective junk:
'I need you. I need you singing
To piece together me';

For, over one doorway, a lifesize stucco
Face of an old man, bearded with a
Strangely bemused look, leans like the carving
On a ship's prow,
Away from old fires and amber streetlamps,
Into the real night of moonlight and wind.

At the edge of my vision, curtains billow,
like sails, on the inside of a window.
A wind enters all the houses I remember
Having lived in through the years. . .

Back home, we sit and read together.
'Daytime,' she keeps insisting, pointing
To the face of the model reclining
In the magazine. 'Night!
Night!' I follow her finger
Through dark swirls of the surrounding hair.

FOG

In London, on the last morning
Of the year, I awoke
To the burning off of the fog,

Wondering again, in contrast, how
The light in Southern France or Provincetown
Could have such a special quality
That painters, drawn to it like flies,
Would cling inverted,
Gaping through its lucid rinse
At each morsel vibrating into the dark
Head like a struck triangle.

High in my 'Clean Air District,'
I stepped from the house into sunlight,
Crossed the freshly steaming road
And stared down the other side of the hill
Into a cloud:
Beached, still, cottony acres of it
Beneath the empty azure sky,
Its whale or camel presence white
And contained as if it were still
Adrift at twenty-thousand feet.

Block by block, descending; eyebeams
Muffled, head swallowed; goggled
In a biplane of bones to enter
The world of fog and frost:

How much it reminded me of that recurrent
Dream I'd gasp in
For that one last breath to strap to me
Before I was plunged into awful fathoms
Or overwhelmed by a sky-falling tidal wave,
Only to find I could breathe in the new
Element like mist! And then, secure,
I'd open up all of my
Dovetailing wings like windows
Of translucent flesh
In generous scoopings and embracings;
Unconscious and reborn,
I'd go like a blossomed dolphin
Through the mothering liquid envelope
Of my phosphorous dream. . .

Now in shivering lungsful of vision
Atomized to pointalism,
Room to see melting before me
Each step cubic with dew, I swung
Through a radiant ash of sunlight
Diffused through protoplasm, almost
Sure that Heaven was
The dislocation of the self.

No color, really, just a fine
Flouring of pastels sifting
Over a whisper of facades,
Snuffing angles, the manmade grown
Incorporeal as haloes;
Intersections floating
Like impressionistic lilies;
Vehicles silvered and mossed together;

Sharply bitten ever-green
Concavities of holly leaves,
Whitened to about the eighth of an inch
A razor blade is honed to,
Loomed in hair-netted hedgefuls
Only to dissolve. . .

Spanning a parted sheet-metal fence,
Ever so slightly furred pure white,
Strands run to a picturebook web. Threaded
Beads of crystal pirouetted
As I bent to it with melting breath.
. . . must be a summer delicacy left over—
What could be caught in late December
But a human eye. . .

Parting the curtains at the edge,
A full-figured mask eclipsed for a moment
The little sun it had let in.
Then, whether pigs have wings. . . . tapping,
Tapping each seedling of reality
Into the pavement with his cane,
An old man waddled past with the
Hurdy gurdy of a nursery rime.

And brushing by, equally blended,
Cloud and clear sky, the moist
Aeriated blue, recharging
Like a pastorale,

Rode me out of my dissolution,
Quickening a white-washed dairy lest
A sail's reflection in the brilliant gulf
Billow open the mind once more.

Up Crouch Hill, I slowly rose
To the surface, blinking out of
Imagination's gills. A ghostly
Full moon overhead, step
By step, became the sun
Until I looked away in pain.
The miracle of Fatima flashed
Through   and was gone.

Slowly, tissues of a dream,
Blown awake and let down
In clarifying sunlight,
Settled on twigs of nuts and bolts;

And like the precarious girder lumber
Floated full-circle by the crane,
I felt in my bones returned to this weathered
Nailed-together maze we share.

APARTMENT 3C

The terrifying angel has come to live with me
He is the color of old meat, hungry birds pass
Over his body like hands
Sexless
Arrogant
He disrobes
Settles himself comfortably under
Floorboard, stands behind the mirror
Soaking up the silver

If he were to make love to me
I would first be prepared like a butterfly
Then tied to the bedpost with umbilical cord
If he were to beat me, the blood
And the bruises would show
Only on the bottoms of my feet
But he will do neither
Crosses his legs in the bedroom chair
Steam surrounding his hairlessness
Saying
Go ahead
You are your own best lover
You are your own tormentor
I am content just to watch

All evening long he turns
The catch on the lock back and forth
After midnight he changes
Into a golden fish
Travels along my spine
Laying eggs in the mucous and the marrow
By morning he has rearranged
The furniture, left fingerprints
On the mahoghany still-born
And suddenly I am sorry for the people who have happened
To me, how I have eaten them up
Spitting out the anchovies
How I have set fire to my hair
So they could watch

The terrifying angel has moved
In, a chilling heat
Surrounds

All that is wooden
And a yawn moves in the apartment, a constant breeze
I confront him,

My nakedness
Unbearable
To the both of us

holy mother
you have not been fair to us
either
we who have

breasts and hair
and cunts like
yours you have
made them afraid
of us
for the reason we look alike
have made them run
from us screaming or in
silence
while at night they drop
tears
on our bellies not
come and grow
beards because they cannot hold a razor
near their throats you have made it
so that we look
like their wives
or we look like you
or we look like women they
have never seen before
you have made them afraid
to touch us is all

holy mother i think
of the poems where i tell
my secret that i want to be
their dancer their ballerina
i think of the night i did dance
on table tops to steam heat
ragtime
and i wanted to go home with and fuck
the piano player but i went home with
and slept just slept
with the carpenter
because you have also made me
afraid
afraid of their fear afraid of
what they are afraid of i wanted
to fuck the piano player but i knew
he would look at my nakedness
and remember you

or look at you
and be turned to stone before my turn came
that is how it would have been and i was afraid
of my own mirror of the way my breasts look moving afraid
of my own dancing i am still

afraid
holy mother
i am trying to tell myself
something i am trying
to give myself
something i am trying
trying like hell but you
keep interfering mother i stand

i kneel before you
i am the only woman in my poems
i am the lady poet fucked
by all and wanted
by none
this is what you have done mother when

you spread for them
and pull off just before they come
when you do your biting
when you take yourself out
on them when you spit
it back into their own
mouths i charge you
when you send them crawling
away grateful only
that you have not smashed
all their bones when you strangle
their hearts with the very bracelets
they have given you holy

mother
do you think
also what you are doing
to your daughters

FURNITURE

My mother and I have been in the attic.
The house gets emptied,
a dancehall,
a bandshell.

Without us, it is so delicate, a balanced skeleton.
In and out of closets and clothing,
we crisscross the afternoon light,
spot it with mauve and yellow.
Looking to the garden she comments
how
the birdbath tilts and she will be gone by the season it fills white.

The average American relocates 2 to 3 times during a 5 year period.

How many springs ago we planted
a dogwood,
a ceremony for something to do with ourselves. She whispers
she will never know when it finally flowers.
I try on wedding dresses of the same spring.
My sister's fits me better now.
Almost naked with my mother, I want her to touch me.
She talks of tissuing both gowns, as if
to dredge some magic from them.
I wait for questions,
she determines her own answers,
I ask her to touch me.

Drapes are cobwebs, fold heavy on the furniture.

My mother knows she will die
traveling,
my father will place her barefoot bones in the Florida sand.
My sister squats, drops subsequent children from her boiled thighs,
while I strain for poems outside myself,
listen to the pauses,
the twists over telephone wire.

Huge and a green, the house relaxes on itself, a fat woman,
becomes sullen, dreamy on birthdays,
holidays.
It is my hair tangled in the mahoghany stain,
my fingerprints like mobiles near the eaves.
My mother plans to appease ghosts with ammonia, dust
vampires off light bulbs, take the chandeliers
with her.

This address is a moment I have lived in.
A swamp, it grows restless and dank in summer.

The house gets emptied. We use a stomach pump.

Doris Radin

SUMMER STORM AT TIORATI
SUDDENLY REMEMBERED

After the rain
the sounds
of the forest
shaking itself off everything
is green—
the green green gets
when it's wet:
I step from rock to rock
over rivulets
turning
to mud; under my feet
I feel the
moss
ooze
I hear

at the foot of the oak
            something
         shoots out
      orange
orange with red
spots
   a newt
now
motionless

jewel set in moss

         *

I line the box
place the

newt in green velvet

I have always feared
being placed in a box
   no matter how

lovingly

32

ABSENCE POEM

for my elder son

The BaMbuti woman
thinks of the forest
is thinking of the forest
all the while she's away
living the life of the village
living in a hut of mud
instead of a hut of leaves
large *mongongo* leaves
that keep out the rain.
The village
where rain comes down
so hard it cuts
and the sun digs pits
       behind each eye
her forest
where the fall of the rain is broken
gentle even in a storm
whose trees join
to make a roof above her head
  orchidsmonkeysbirds.
the smell of leaf mold.
soft green light.
         she drinks
water from the streams
cool, clear, sweet
(village water is dirty
has a bitter taste.)
she washes the sweat
from her body, sweat from the hunt
from beating the nets.
To wake in the forest to the song
song of the *molimo*
to walk along the antelope trail
gathering mushrooms
to hear the chameleon's long sad call
and know tomorrow's
hunt for honey will go well,
to get drunk on *apuma*
dance to the rhythm of the *ngbengbe* sticks
all the while
all the while
she's away from it

THE COAT

soft
my arms through the sleeves
I have buttoned the buttons
turned
the collar up   I am sitting
on my bed
      in the dark

                  brown coat my coat
I keep it always
on the top of the closet
in a large white box, my coat
is wrapped
in tissue
today I have
taken it out
it is
dark brown
and heavy my coat
I have it so long I no longer
remember
when I got it
but I know it is
always there
on the top of my closet
wrapped,
and if I have taken it
out of its box
    on and off
all the years I can remember
it does not show,
the nap
is deep;
and if today I
wrap
myself in its dark I know
that tomorrow
or the next day
                  or the next

PINNED IN THE CENTER OF THE EYE

such pain
Midas must have felt
when his daughter his golden haired
daughter when she was
turning to gold at that moment
he sees her, a thing of feathers
flying, trying to escape
into the blue of her eye—
he watches
        the tips   then the whole wing. . .
pinned there in the center of her eye,
his pain
And William Tell as he aimed,
apple on his son's head,
eye steady on the apple
slowly
draws his bow   the boy's head
his small son's head so large
at that moment
                an image blinds him
arrow hurtling through the air
brains
        caught on the end of it
how can I tell you

FOR MY FATHER

(1896-1956)

A stillness
moments before dark
stillness so
still it can be heard
in the bones
of trees
in air as it turns
the color of lead
a man
deep in his heavy
coat, collar turned up
hands in his pockets
faces an empty
bench,
his dark figure
stands to the side of it,
a question mark
· at the end of a sentence
        Bending toward the bench
              his good ear
listens, but not to the
quiet. . .
someone is speaking

from the bench:
Louis, I find you lacking
light-heartedness, my darling,
you're a turtle hiding
head and all
come out from under
      your impenetrable
shell, look at the shining world.*

And she dead these months,
taken in her prime,
yea sayer
helpmeet
sunshine of his life
these her words
plea carved on his shell
a quarter of a century ago

36

still it can be
heard in the bones
of trees
in air as it turns
the color of coal
the man shrinks
        into his pockets
In the light of the gaslamp
his shadow
a long shadow
        heard in the bones
of trees, in the air as it turns
a quarter of a century later:
Days of affliction have taken hold upon me.
In the night season my bones are pierced in me,
And the pains that gnaw me take no rest.
By the great force of my disease
is my garment disfigured:
It bindeth me about as the collar of my coat. . .
And I am become like dust
and ashes.

1975

*

From a letter written by Rose Bonfield (1902-1952)
to her husband, May 1, 1923

Quotation from The Book Of Job

AFTERNOONS

The drunken butterflies sip on the lips of flowers
    with opening and shutting wings
with opening and shutting wings, they sit, the drunken
      butterflies
    their colors opening and shutting.
I can think of nothing else but these butterflies
    with opening and shutting wings
        : so beautiful

The dying flies are spinning madly on the ledge
    with flapping and buzzing bodies
with flapping and buzzing bodies, they spin, the dying
      flies
    their bodies spinning and buzzing.
I can think of nothing else but these flies
    with spinning and buzzing bodies
        : so dreadful

OCTOBER SONG

They who never ruled before
                    poured from their factory districts
                    across the bridges of Petrograd
            to make October.
The moon was so startled
            all global tides
        shifted.
The lights went on all over Europe.
                    Nothing
            can ever be the same.

NEW DAY

The moon is setting.
On either side a broken tank.
Besides the tanks black mushrooms.
The sky is bright.
     That is all.

The sun is rising.
On either side a shattered rifle.
Besides the rifles red mushrooms.
The sky is bright.
     That is all.

LONGING

Hard as I resist
    when I see our father rising
    to kiss his great painted lady
my thoughts fly to you.

     When our cousin comes at night
     with all his brilliant children
I am sitting before my lodge.

      Can you hear me sighing?

MORNING

We rise, we rise
We, whose dances make the earth to tremble.

We rise, we rise
We, in whose thighs there is power.

We rise, we rise
We, who let our hair grow long in rage.

We rise, we rise
We, in whose throat a song is always leaping.

We rise, we rise
,We, whose unruly beards embellish the dawn.

GROSS FREIHEIT STRASSE

where the strippers jam plastic cocks
            up their cunts
        while good burghers wait to see doings
            in brass cages & leather corsets
                bars where the girls are really guys
        and bars where the girls were guys
non-stop sexorama in 1970's Reich
                gruppen sex & porno film
        seventy-seven bars every three blocks
            erotic gardens
    where young whores peddle
            from pegboard stalls
                    challenging the old pros
                        stuck in the streets of windows
        until Van Gogh's grinning ear
    falls dripping upon the Hamburg stage
and an old stripper goes beserk
        shoving dildoes up every ass hole
            angels in leather
    let their audiences have it
            with cat o nine tails
        the women who wrestle in mud
suddenly flip all the sailors into the sea
        faggots murder their best customers
    bars burn
    neons explode
erotic gardens erupt
        an army of skeletons from Dachau
    puts the city under siege
    a hail of Auschwitz teeth
                batters the frantic bodies
        still fucking in the streets
                and my hand slips from its wrist
            crawls down the wall
                    to a room below
        where it liberates a pistol
                to carry to a comrade
            calling out
                my name

FROM THE MAD WIFE'S ROOM IN JANE EYRE

I only knew mother naked
when father was out
and the servants cunningly
hidden elsewhere in the house.

Through the keyhole
I watched her undress.
The shadow of banana leaves
wandered along her breasts.
Slowly, to watch herself emerge.

With nipples erect
under her fingers
she would sigh, throw back her head,
hair curling down her like heat waves.
And laugh.
Loudly.

How she teased herself
from the hair down
the feet up
until she could stand no more
and folded to the floor
beneath the window
opening her legs
wide, to the sunlight and her hand.
How she laughed
into that final backward somersault
before lying still
her face guarded from sun
by banana leaves.

One day, when I, too,
was laughing with legs open to the sun
she entered my room,
kissed me, "Yes,
Bertha. That is right.
That is who we are."

How we laughed in the sunlight
with the windows open.
Down below
men shook their heads
muttering, "women's gossip."

Soon after they took her away.
Nurse started dressing me:
roughly tugging night clothes over day clothes,
scratching dresses over nightgowns
kept firmly on while her harsh red hands
scrubbed between my legs. . .
never lingering
as she hitched my head up
her tight eyes away
whenever skin must show.

She never knew about hands,
or noon, she never laughed,

never knew about nights
when she snored
on the other side of my bed
nightcap tied firmly,
her coarse nightgown
clamped between her feet,

never knew about moonlight;
how, with breasts growing,
I fingered them, like mother,
silently learning her loud laugh;
how I heaped pillows on the floor
under the window
curtains drawn slightly back,
sprawled under the dark banana shadows
with the full moon
guiding my hands
circling, circling. . .

Then I met him.
Oh so ugly. Walking as if carrying
a jar of importance on his head.
But somewhere in his eyes
I thought I saw my mother's curling hair
and how I felt his loud laugh
like heat waves rising.

Laced in, corsetted, be-jewelled
I was signed over to him by father
with my thirty thousand pounds.

I couldn't help it
that just two weeks after we were married
it was full moon;
that he didn't snore as loudly as nurse;
that, though he silenced my laughing in his bed,
I couldn't stop laughing alone with the moonlight
my naked body, my hand, circling, circling. . .
and oh how I couldn't resist
after fourteen nights of being held down,
couldn't resist that lovely somersault.

It was worth it.
In spite of how he slapped me,
almost strangled me flat
as he opened my legs
and yelled "no"
whenever my body moved,
his eyes dulled now
like his hands
and the silence.
Then we left Jamaica.

The English doctors
made me sleepy,
laid me down
under the inlaid leaves
on their white ceilings.

I remembered mother
as their fingers wandered
between my legs
gentler than my husband
and I heard her laugh
saw again the hot sun
and her long warm hair

Oh they knew how to stroke me
circling, circling. . .

then stopped
shoving my legs together,
waking me,
their hands shaking
as they glared down
with full hard eyes.

Yesterday he locked me in this room.
Even in England he couldn't still me.
Especially at noon, hour of my mother.
Especially at full moon.

The grey bricks scratch here
unhung with tapestries
and no sound seeps through
that foot thick door.
It doesn't smell of living
just that old woman's stale gin
and my unwashed skin.

But at last, there's a milky sun
in this damp English sky
and she's drunk again,
snoring like poor old nurse.

Off with this dress.
Are you ready, Mother?

BONDING

That Saturday
cycling to Brownies
wearing my first new watch

I knew he needed the time
when he smiled

I saw:

no sweets
not even dolls
dangling from his pockets

just his watchless hands
lost inside his raincoat

I braked
raised my wrist

where do you live he whispered

*half past just
down the road*

will you go away with me he invited
bald with a stained front tooth

and I knew where he lived
hands moving in his raincoat
like those men
I'd seen
by the paddling pool,
wondering if my father did it
in the bathroom
trying to see through the keyhole
watching if he wore a raincoat
under his dressing gown

I knew:

yes was wrong
no was rude
I must look him in the eyes
not at his absent hands

I didn't think of father
giver-of-permission
as one hand left his coat
for my handlebars but
mumbled
I'll have to ask my mother first.

THE DEATH OF LOTTIE SHAPIRO

how old were you mother?
thirty-seven
I'm almost that now
What did they take
your right breast
or your left
I don't remember
did I ever know
you were little
weren't you
in your red robe
and silver slippers
I loved you
your fingers smelled from cigarettes
I loved the smell
talk to me mommy
look at me
with eyes
that stare into the kitchen air
and you smoke
and drink your coffee
I drink coffee too.

I was eleven that day
you gave me a brownie camera
and then you went away
and the house got echoes
and it wasn't comfortable there anymore
I walked the stairs stairs
to see you and you looked at me
from your bed and were glad to see me
and you saw me from your bed
you wore a rubber breast in your empty cup
my cup runneth over
you saw my big breasts
I was seventeen
and you went again
how stupid to repeat a nightmare
and we rode you and I
in an ambulance
and you were glad to go
you were hurting so
and I said
I'm proud of you

What the hell did I mean
proud you never screamed
or banged your head
or pulled my breasts
proud of your quiet
quiet
quiet
quiet
obscene whispers in the hall
the nurse was saying
that is all
she didn't know you
that goddamn nurse
my mother was diseased
your face was white
and then the hairs grew
and you still bathed and combed
and put on pretty gowns
and we came
my sister and me
we came to visit
and fed you ginger ale
and you died kindly
you died asking
how is?
how is?
    . . . fine . . fine . .
why didn't you scream
did you know there was no one to answer you
what did you think about
propped on three pillows
and your sister came
to watch you die
and we visited
my sister and me
we tried to share
we took turns
brought you things
got and got
talked and
talked
to doctor doctor doctor ears
and in the shower I screamed
and in my car I screamed
I screamed for you
you couldn't scream
you were being kind dying
screaming wasn't your style
and one day you said

51

it was hard to brush your teeth
and I wanted to scream at you
YOU HAVE TO BRUSH YOUR TEETH YOU HAVE TO
YOU KEPT GINGER ALE DOWN YOU ARE NOT GOING
    TO DIE.
You are not going to die
and you did
I saw you
in your bedroom tomb
lying on your bed
same bed
old bed
and daddy said
I think she's dead
lying on your bed
same bed
old bed
and daddy said
I think she's dead

and I looked at you
and you weren't you
and I was scared looking at you
weren't you
and your white gown didn't quite cover
and your breasts no breasts
and your face
not face
and my mommy
not my mommy
and the air out of a balloon
and you looked
so not like you
and my sister said
that's not mommy
and of course, it wasn't
and only the doctor cried
he said you wanted to live
he cried and we didn't
we didn't know how
and anyhow it takes a long time
to know people are dead.

INDEPENDENTLY HEALTHY . . . FOR DR. SHAPIRO AND ME

how will I know when the day's here
you will be standing on your head under the airconditioner
the artificial roses will get soft and some will die

I will remember the painting over the couch (the decorator said it
                                                           matched)
there will be no kleenex boxes

you will offer me scotch
and we will talk for 56 minutes
(You will pay for half the time)

you will tell me about your daughter's boy friend
your wife's father
how your mother
never seemed to be at home

there will be a rumba band (playing softly)
and I will say
        do you remember Carmen Miranda?

and when it's almost time to go
you will hand me
an old picture
(I'll barely recognize)

and I'll laugh and say

        oh sure . . sure. . . .

aunt rose
    institutionalized
after the abortion I think

hunched in the front seat
    window
                part of a cheese sandwich

car sick
my mother's dress from another year

I sat right in back
    of her
and looked
didn't look
as she vomited her normalcy

        on the way back
and forever after

I would worry
about being crazy.

13.

white gal carol

steppenwolf fetchit
boogies wif miz ann
th mains regret
petals french.

no mo black bitch
songs blue sea,
            soft black
mama   fed me   mama.

dozens for y'all
blackface women.

33.

outlaw of the jingle

if you fail to make poems full
blown opals of evil myth,
say, that Eve, *jung fraulein,* well-
endowed, and Adam, are both
beasts of man and woman;
and if you fail to summon
(in guise of socialist rev)
the demons we all conceal,
then, hmmm you will never do
for New York Times Book Review.

35.

first kingdom

for mary emily hunter

there are no daisies.
shaggymane mushrooms

push through the live brain
dead with the fever

in the marrow of
the soul, and the flesh

drip slow off bone, drops
of cold amoeba.

39.

poets readn

Labor Day, 1975

so we won't let the water
fall and not write something in
to honor the occasion
we work in as a language
we're in for better or worse.

we have a politics and
ethics in which we harness
powers like the falls, good, yes
paterson, that's in the past.

well we get up talk and read
as like each ripple the great
noise of the water fall drowns.

44.

medium

tom, a black ghost, white
like haunts which nightly
moan self righteous lust

moonlight dark meat to
writhe beyond the pale
english of braille flesh.

37.

love program

for s.e.c.

butch the mechanic sings
a brighter day t.v.
and late night radio
her old sofware routines
from raw data you see
as the world turns much too slow.

orbits moon for a spell
to compute the language
of cloned will amplified
through the solid state cell
as the wave front image
of lightning deified.

there is a crankcase
filled wif oil for the good
halflife rust of desire
in her chrome paradise
blest by an idling god
of thick smoke and thin fire.

Carole Stone

VISITING MY GRANDMOTHER

Side by side like two numbed cats
my brother and I sat,
while the trolley ground its gears
up the dark street
where my grandmother lived
on the second floor.
Photos of our dead mother and father
hugged her wall.

Two lovebirds watched her ladle soup
into heavy red flowered dishes.
Giving us bread without butter,
she wiped tears from her eyes.
"Shaineh maiddeleh," she intoned,
"Shain kindelach."
My brother ate and ate
I hardly touched my plate.
After twelve potato pancakes,
he was her hero.

Silently we watched her second husband
drink his schnapps, belch,
and slurp his soup through his teeth;
"Mister," my grandmother told him,
"Be nice."

ABOUT ME

There are some things I like
about my life
getting up in the morning
alone
drinking coffee while
reading the *New York Times*
going back to bed if I want to.

There are even seasons
when I feel good
for no special reason—
the rhythms are right.
I watch trees a lot
when they are bare
and wait patiently
for Spring.

The sky is best for me
when it is pink at 5 p.m.
In summer I drive past tennis courts
and look at mens' bodies.
In winter I make reservations
to go to exotic places
and cancel them.

On birthdays
I still like my body
my thin face
with its high cheekbones.

I'm not happy.

MOMENTO

Forever frozen
in Sloppy Joe's
Havana,
1938
my parents sip Cuba Libres —
a handsome couple.

My father's black hair
pomaded and polished
is parted in the middle.
He wears white pants
a navy blue double breasted blazer
and smokes a cigar —
el jefe.

Delicately, my mother
balances her self
tanned and smiling
elegant in a polka dot gown
and mink wrap.
A velvet cloche hides
half her profile.

Always I've tried to imagine
her full face
to guess the thoughts
behind those clear eyes
staring past me.

In the background
a stranger
caught by the camera
hunches over the bar
sucking on the ice
in his banana daquiri.

Years I've spent
inventing his case-history
making him a go-between
for the gambling syndicate
and my father,
my mother's lover,
a narcotics agent.

Years I've treasured
this cheap souvenir photo
of their honeymoon
reminding me of their deaths.

GOING AWAY FANTASY

The faces of the two children
I love
will be thick with surprise.
"I am going away,
leaving you."

Astonished they will pick
at red spaghetti
with reluctant forks
thinking, "Mothers do not run
away from home."

As if still small, they will ask
for milk with chocolate syrup,
icecream and cookies
to sweeten this quick rush
of blind parting—
so slow in coming.

We used to travel together
to the Emerald City.
Guarding them against winged monkeys
flying out from the yellow
dining room curtains,
I beat back the Wicked Witch
of the West.

Now my boy and girl
almost grown
are safe rooted by my roots—
I am lost again.

PEREGRINACION

I awaken remembering our nights.
We are like turtles
emerging from mud
as los penitentes
get up at dawn
to begin their pilgrimage
from San Miguel
to San Juan dos Lagos.

When the man with a trumpet shouts
"Santa Maria!"
sleeping men, women, and children
rise from the fields
and file behind his banner
of red and gold
to walk the roads to forgiveness.

We too will follow him
to the church at Atotonilco
where pilgrims flagellate themselves
in narrow cells.
We will walk with barefoot women
carrying babies in torn rebozos

climb stony hillsides
as wind blows through our shirts
stumble over spiny cactus
sending semaphore messages.

Searching for the river
we will find crows whistling in dead trees.
At dusk you will gather firewood
as I make our bed of straw.
When you hold me in the dark
I will be calm.

Like tortoises we will crawl away
from the old loneliness.

How far it is to grace.

Penny Bihler

HIROSHIGE: WOMEN IN A BATH-HOUSE

The old woman bends
her sharp right elbow,
rubs at her crotch.

The young mother squats,
breasts flopping forward,
to soap her daughter's face.

Two round barrels
by her buttocks,
another scrubs her friend's spine
with a dripping rag.

A baby's fat legs
squirm on her mother's belly.

The old woman grins,
lathers a hairy calf
with her left hand.

The floorboards are rectangular.

THE PIGEON MAN [AND THE PIGEON LADY]

The pigeon man
hates pigeons.

Unlike the pigeon lady
who daily waddles boulevards
with her bag of bread crumbs,
leaving a trail of droppings,
clucking softly
at the root of her tongue,

the pigeon man
is silent.

His muscled haunches
are hardened
from climbing into belfreys.
His fingers do not twitter
but curl to hold the eggs
in their bony cradle.

And he gathers the eggs,
and he gathers the eggs
for the boiling,
the evening boiling,
the ritual of bubbles
as the pigeon embryos
writhe a bit
and stiffen
to hot deaths
in his copper pots.

In the morning
he climbs again
to put them back
in emptied nests,
to put them back.

He descends the iron-runged ladders
whistling.

He passes the pigeon lady.
They do not speak,
though he has been plotting
to climb to her nest
for years now.

Someday he will boil
the last egg
and it will be all over
for the pigeon man
the pigeon lady

and the final puzzled pigeon,
brooding,
wearing a permanent
egg-shaped hole
into the pale underfeathers
of her beating breast.

THE HOLLOW CONTAGION

1.

Looking out of their photographs
the poets' eyes dilate
to seize us fiercely.

Their folded hands
in quiet laps
twitch
saying
> love me
> know me
> I am here
> oh let us touch

and the cry
always the cry
rises
a vertigo of need
and our ancient ritual
of naming
begins.

2.

It is a hollow contagion
a reverse pregnancy
body swelling with hunger
space vast and desperate
for the kick
or the kicks
of life.

And the bones of the ribs
part for the heart's quickening
and the bones of the forehead
burst against the skin
till the woman opens her legs
again
> and
> > again
for the poem
and all her dark mouths come

till the man grows erect
for want of the poem
and comes as he can
his rhythm
his vital spurts
come home
            come home

and still the poem
screams
            love me
            know me
            I am here
            oh let us touch
and still
it is not
enough.

3.

In the Steichen photograph
the room is black.
A woman
who is only a woman
sits in the middle
of a long slatted bench.
We cannot see her face.
Her knees are drawn up
to her chin
and her head drives deep
into her tight crossed arms.
We hear her heart beating.

She hears
            her heart
                        beating.
Her arms
            are locked
                        across her knees.
Her feet are bare
            toes curling
                        over the wooden edge.
What does she want?

Who does she love?

Have all the sidewalks of her life
led only to holding herself
alone
in this black room?

4.

It is a hollow contagion
this tribal rite
        of words
                    we speak here
stuttering truths
        out the holes
                    of our mouths
as our hands tremble
        smooth the paper
                    reach for one another.

There are orphans in the world
cold in their cribs
cold
    even
        in their mother's arms.

Toi Derricotte

THE MIRROR POEMS

Je vous livre le secret des secrets.
Les miroirs sont les portes par
lesquelles la Mort va et vient.

—*Jean Cocteau*

Prologue:

If she could only break the glass—
the silver is already peeled back like first skin
leaving a thin
transparent thing that floats across the ground
in front of her : this white shadow.

1. what a mirror thinks

   _____

   a mirror thinks it has no self
   so it wants to be everything it sees

   it also thinks everything is flat

   put a bunch together
   & they think they see
   the back side of the moon

2. the mirror as a judge of character

   _____

   keening my appetite
   on the taste of an image of myself
   sharpening myself
   on bones;
   suddenly
   i lean over its eye
   & see the way i see myself

   i ask it
   am i fairest in all the land

it opens like a backwards lake
& throws out of its center
a woman
combing her hair
with the fingers of the dead

3. the mirror & suicide

_____

someday
stand before a mirror & feel
you are drowned

let
your hair spread as sweet Ophelia's did
& you will rock
back & forth
gently
like a boat in kind water

4. questions to ask a mirror

_____

remember:
whatever you ask a mirror
it will ask back

if you ask it
what will you give me
it will ask you
what will you give me

if you ask it what is love
it will turn into a telescope
& point at you

if you ask it what is hate
it will do the same thing

if you ask it what is truth
it will break in nine pieces

if you ask it what is beauty
it will cast no reflection

if you ask it to show you the world
it will show you the eye of your mother

5. conversing with the mirror

———————————————

never tell a mirror you are black
it will see you as a rainbow
never tell a mirror you are white
it will make you disappear
in fact a mirror doesn't care
what color you are

never tell a mirror
how old you are
under 20
you draw a blank
over 40 it stares

never cry in front of a mirror
it gets cruel

if a mirror doesn't trust you
it squints

if a mirror hates you
it speaks in a high-pitched voice

if a mirror calls you long distance
don't accept charges hang up

never run from a mirror
it always leaves a friend outside

never have sex with a mirror
you will have in-grown children

don't take money from a mirror
there are strings

if you must converse with a mirror
say to it: you're pretty
& won't get broken

that gives you
7 years

6. the mirror & time
_____

the mirror IS NOT immortal
in fact it only has nine lives:

the first one is a thief
the second a baker
the third plays the harpsichord
the fourth lives in the iron-bound
section of newark &
eats pork sausage
the fifth predictably drinks
the sixth goes into the convent
but the seventh (this gets better)
marries her father
& humps up like a camel
the eighth cries a lot & ZAP
changes into a writer

7. the mirror & metamorphosis
_____

the eye   in the mirror   is the mirror   of the eye

8. the mirror & the new math
_____

inside the mirror
opens up like the number zero
you swim around in there
bob up
& drown
like the rat in Wonderland's flood.

your tail would like to hook a reason,

but you keep coming
face to face
breast to breast
with yourself.

you fall backwards & away, even
think that you are lost
in Oceanic O,

but you are still
pinned to an inverse.

9. the mirror as a silent partner

_____

the mirror never talks
it is always astounded
with its O mouth open
& everything falling in

Epilogue:

Always straining toward her image, the girl
let go.

Tentacles of light
unlocked
like hooks of parasite

& she came back
in dark so dark,

she cannot see by sight

UNBURYING THE BIRD

buried birds
are usually
dead.
fallen from the sky
because of too much
something.
      too much high.
      too much steep.
      too much long.
      too much deep.
but sometimes
one has been known
to go underground.
you do not hear a peep
for years.
then one day,
you go back to the spot
thinking you will not find
a feather   or a few
scattered bones
& you hear something
pecking   trying
to get out of there.
you are afraid to believe
it is still alive.
afraid that even if it is
in freeing it, it will die.
still,
slowly,
you go about freeing the bird.
you scrape away the grave
which in some mysterious way
has not suffocated her.
you free her scrawny head.
her dangling wing.
you keep thinking her body
must be broken beyond healing.
you keep thinking the delicate
instruments of flight
will never pull again.
still,
you free her.
feed her from the tip of your finger.
teach her the cup of your hand.

you breathe on her.
one day,
you open up your hand
& show her sky.

A DANDELION

The fluffs of a dandelion
    fly away on the wind
My mother is at home in Nichinan

Her husband died
    burnt a thin smoke in the sky
Her second daughter is at home with her
    she says she won't marry
Her first and fifth sons are fishermen
    they spend most of the year on the sea
Her first daughter is in Takarazuka
    there are 300 miles between Takarazuka and Nichinan
Her second son is in Osaka
    there are 300 miles between Osaka and Nichinan
Her sixth son is in Tokyo
    there are 500 miles between Tokyo and Nichinan
Her third son is in Lisbon
    there are 6,500 miles between Lisbon and Nichinan
Her fourth son is me in Duluth
    there are 8,000 miles between Duluth and Nichinan

When I left home last time
she saw me off standing on the platform
like the stem of a dandelion.

THE MUSHROOMS OF THE SUBWAY

two lines of pale light of the rails of the subway
stretch far into the dark depths of the tunnel

by the rails at the side of the platform
mushrooms are growing in a spot
dark and clumsy like a lump of dog shit
                                        growing
in the mud of oil and iron filings
in the color of the mud

the trains scatter the oil and iron filings over them
                                        over and over
the heavy shrieks of the wheels pierce them
                                        mushrooms
broken and exposing the white insides of powdery bones
then get rotten down and return to the oily mud
                                        again
the trains blow away the spores.

RHAPSODY ON A THEME FROM PAGANINI,
BY RACHMANINOFF

in a cool and
    clear forest
        making fire of
            birch bark and leaves
the perfume of the fire
    permeates the air
        brandy in the glass gains
            the warmth of the palm

gathering the leaves
    in the garden
        is found
            a ring of yesterday

sitting in
    a little white chair
        I read a letter
            of the past
the dark eyes do not luster
    any more
        in the peace of twilight

from the window
    the music flows through
        the falls near the garden
            flow serenely
the fallen leaves flowing
    listlessly in the stream
        into the lake
            to depart to a far coast

fall, fall
    your falling leaves
        scatter
            in the depths of my heart
I write a letter
    on the fallen leaves
        send it to
            the hurt of the depths.

THE VENUS

I was swimming in the bottom of the sea
the sun was on the surface
    the rays piercing the lucid blue water
the pattern of the waves was waving
    on the white sands of the bottom
schools of red and green fish were playing
    around the coral and seaweed
Swimming among them
    I saw a shadow moving on the sands of the bottom
I looked up and floated toward the surface
    the water turned warm around me
the shadow was the Venus
    with no top or bottom
        the pubic hair was waving in the water
I pressed my body up against her
the warm water swirled around us and supported us
    I went into her
it might be the way in which
the dolphin and whale make love in the ocean
I saw no change on her face
    she was gazing into my eyes
I was caught in her lustrous melting eyes
I finished my joy in the sprinkling light
the sun came down over her head and blinded my eyes
    I felt she left me in the foam
I found my body floating in the pattern of the waves
    my body was driven ashore

I threw myself down on the hot sands of the beach
and when I woke up there was nobody around
my back was burning in the evening breeze
I was wondering in my dim shadow
how she could swim with no arms.

There is a big rock
    sticking up in the falls
People call it the man in the falls
    his face looking slightly upward
It reminds me of
    the unfinished statues of Easter Island
but I think the man is older
    than those of Easter Island, where some men
        came from space to carve them
      and ordered them to stand and walk
  so they moved into the field where they are now
       When the men went back to space
they left some unfinished statues in the mountain
    but I know the spacemen did not carve
      the man in the falls
    like an eastern monk who trains himself
        in the icy falls
          day after day
           alone
      in the deep mountain
   he won't quit before he sees the mountain move
But the man in the falls is a clumsy saint of meditation
having been sitting there from long before Dharma Buddha
whose legs shrunk away after his three year sitting
      on the stone
    the man in the falls has no legs or arms
    but has the power of the Balzac by Rodin

When I went to the falls after we had rains for
      a week
the ears of the man were almost covered under the
      flooding water
    he was shaking in the
      heavy flow
And today it was a typical nice day in November
I went to see the man
The water was falling on his shoulders
on which I found some fallen leaves.

THE ANNIVERSARY

Of course we failed, by succeeding.
The fiery cherub becomes his smothering,
The greedy heart dives into a dream
Of power, or truth, and wakes up middle aged
In some committee room.
It is eating paper instead of god.
We two are one, my bird, this is a wedding.

When love was war, you swore you'd burn
Your life and die at thirty-five. I said good riddance,
Bright hairy boy, I will beat you, down,
Tear you to monkey shreds, survive like earth,
Owl-eyed, because I wanted to see everything
Black and permanent and kill you with your theories.
We used to wake up sweaty and entangled.

Thirty, home, and work. We cohabit in a functioning machine.
There is violence, somewhere else. Do we wish this? It occurs,
The flayed combatant, the dismembered child,
The instruments in the basement. We must wish it. See,
Between us is peace, our babies are plump,
I know you, I caress you, I fail you. My faith adheres
In nothing. Don't leave me. Don't leave me.

THE ASTRONOMER'S MATE

Wives of great men all remind us
We can make our lives sublime
And, departing, leave behind us
Sootprints on the hands of Time.

You lie in your obnoxious undershirt
Thinking about the job
You have to unpeel far suns
And become famous.
It is after dinner, you are about to fall asleep
But I do not hit you with a block,
Head of equations, cosmos problem dreamer,
I speak sweetly. It is not what the movies and novels
Led me to expect. It is all effort,
All uphill, always hopeless. We are true.
Tongue, pump, hand, eye.

So have another beer, honey.
The ticker's thudding hard, and the harder
It labors, the quicker clots. Those big red stars
Called giants thunder a mere hundred million
Years of perpetual core explosion
Using up hydrogen. When the heat's off,
A body dies. A body's beauty dies.
Pressure and energy to bulge them, like
The stupid wars we need to keep us up,
Brandishing rods of knowledge, painted bowls,
To rule, to catch, the spiral stellar tails,
The spill of dragon's breath, they finish.

Let us suppose those conflagrations wish
To burn forever. As we have told the doctor,
Our family histories are heart troubled.
That kills our people off, if they are lucky;
Worse jests, if not. Be famous, love. Live long.
Perform. Up we go, then, upstairs, to bed,
To fight again another day.

Lord, lord, it's time to pray.
Entropic One, freezer of galaxies,
King of White Dwarfs, unscrupulous Absence, hear me.
You see this spectacled wonder and myself?
May we become a toddling old couple.
May we make quaint appearance at weddings and funerals.

May we be a curiosity
Until wood splinters in the bowels of dragons,
Until the pitcher shivers at the well-curb,
Until the pump clogs. Understand me now.
Let neither of us tend the other's cancer,
But race for whose heart stops first, his or mine.

ELEGY

December 20, 1965

What may I tell? The sharp death that does not leave
nor rich men nor high: it him took.

　　　　　　　　　—Saxon Chronicle

i

In Doom Year, the day of his number,
My sole striding father was humbled.
His heart hurt a moment, he fell vacated,
And hit that sidewalk, if there is mercy, dead.

ii

These are my visions: knife vision driving
Alone towards you the given stiffclothes bittercold man
Around whom vertical overcoats gaze
Horrified, gluttonous, breathing—
And vision in the hospital basement
While the dirty balding coroner jokes,
You and I meet, who never meet again,
Although I establish unalterably glassed
Hard forehead's breadth from temple to temple,
Sleeping eyes, left tightened cheek bruised brown,
Ironic mouth that speechlessly bids me
Stay with you, be eternal.
And vision of the burning
While we prayed to the spider God
And screamed behind our eyelids,
The boxed brainpot, depository
Of school verse and love's future gesture
Takes fire, steams, the diffident tongue is eaten,
The racing leg collapses,
The tender life of testicles withers,
Now the marrowbones lose their juice,
Now the teeth and vertebrae drop
Glowing, incandescent among cinders,
At last the stubborn clotted heart is punished,
While we sleepwalk from the chapel to the car
Quiet now, quiet now
Quiet now he is burning no more.

iii

Must not the widow pass strange hours,
Having lain beside one man forever,
Having his odors still in the house,
Having us love one another because we grieve?

iv

Curse this. All our lives swear hatred
Of the abominable enemy, that
Is the condition of our breath, and yet
Now no rage rises, why, no anger,
No outburst, why, but we are anchored
To quietude, as if a stranger
From the deep night entered a room
Blinking shyly at our bright lights,
Who, before anyone spoke to him,
Returned alone into his snowy night
As in tales the wild bird goes, takes flight.

talking about childhood wishes

i find him in a box outside the a & p
his head twice the size of his body
taking him home anyway
buying expensive goat milk
thinking a change in diet may improve
his condition   i don't dare tell
my husband so i hide him under the sofa
i feed him every two hours & change his diapers
i cuddle him & let him nurse even though i
am dry   when he doesn't grow i try to fill
him up with an air pump it doesn't work
i take to wandering the street
in my nightgown, one day i meet the candy man
on the corner of hudson boulevard in jersey city
he gives me a pin striped pill
i crush the pill &
give it to him with an eye dropper
the next day when i look under the sofa he has
turned into ten little men perfectly formed
but only an inch tall   i have a good time letting
them roam my body some sleep in my ear
i move their home to under the tub
one night after i dream i have killed
the lone ranger i drown them

accident

cruising in front of me
the black hearse
with dingy gray drapes
stops me dead

        my license number
        is on the fender

   i pull out in front of it
   forcing the bearded chauffeur
   off the road

"i demand you open the coffin" i said

i see the triangular orange eyes
steel helmets riveted over her breasts
red threads folded in her lap
her crisp chicken legs

       "what happened" i asked

"her brakes failed" he said

now the cat &
              his mother live together

he wore thick glasses with silver rims
the top of his head was bald
with thin hair draped
over his ears
& nape curling at the edges

            the only woman
            he'd ever known
            was his mother &
            they lived together

he worked for Thompson Funeral Home
where he met beautiful Rosa
her jet black hair hugging
her ivory face

      that night he slept with her
      read *Crime & Passion*
            confessed he'd been in a mental
            institution after committing
            sodomy with his mother's cat

held her cool hand on impulse
he pulled down the sheet
& kissed her frozen nipple

                  in the morning
                  his colleagues
                  found him split

                  in half
                  on the autopsy table

it says Joe on your name tag

it says Joe

i see you walking your dog-bodied child
on a leash
to protect him from people paws

on your name tag

rapist   threatening me with a knife
then passing out when i grab &
      ram it in my chest

it says Joe on your name tag

you bald business maggot
feeling my leg under the table
a cigar in one hand
my cunt in the other

it says it all on your name tag Joe

sitting near me at the Jolly Apple

unshaven   fly open

you tell me i'm fat & ugly
& smell like a whore

i puke in your booze

for my son

my seven year rib
sticking in my liver
my black child
in an all
white neighborhood
painted birds pluck
your kinky hair for worms
even the farmer in delaware
won't buy you for 3 chickens
you ask if night has to be dark
then set fire to my study

come

she said come to the magic shop
she said what will you give up for attention?
i said my soul
someone's head snapped back and fell in her lap
the other one said laughingly what is your soul?
someone told my husband it's your wife or death!
her pink legs swung off the bed,
diving into the hole, i heard him screaming
kill me then
i said i will take off my clothes for attention
i will tell you every thought bored she drank
another scotch & water
she said doesn't he look like tiny tim & i said
imagine licking his teeth with your tongue
i said i feel no moral obligation
towards the vietnamese and my children
are starving on candy bars and they're
going to eat our food and
she said you're getting off the track again
what i want is for you to lose 50 pounds &
i said you always do this to me when i'm
stuck with a lousy sandwich
in my hand &
i'm
empty

Malas granata is a tre þat bereth pommegarnettes.
    Trevisa, Barth. De P. R. XVII, 1398.

Pleasant liquor that distils from the pomgranet fine.
    Drayton, Harmonie of Ch., 1591.

With deeper red the pomegranate glows.
    Pope, Odyss. VII, 1725.

POMEGRANATE

1. 0 for a pomegranate —
            firm reddish rind,
            moist crimson pulp,
            & on my tongue,
                    tart garnet nectar.

2. It is not simple,
    selecting an apple garnade.
    Squeezing the thick-skinned berry
    will not penetrate its mystery.
    So take a chance; slice it,
    expose the seeds nestled in a golden honeycomb,
    bite in, take a mouthful,
    taste the bittersweet rush,
    spit the spent seeds,
    lick the ambrosia from dripping fingers.

3. O fecund fruit,
    delectable berry,
    I scatter your seeds.

    If you love me
    let one
    grow
    to be
    a pomegranate
    tree

HAPPY BIRTHDAY AMERICA

July 4, 1976
sitting on the balcony
on the 19th floor of The Green House
in Fort Lee, New Jersey
watching the Tall Ships
sailing down the Hudson
eating watermelon & canteloupe
drinking champagne
& talking to Allen
a vegetarian pimp
about the aesthetics of the business
& how he never fucks his girls
& how they come to him with their problems
(& vice versa)
while the *Esmeralda*
floats by
virgin white
in full sail

It is as if the modern mind, wishing
always to verify its emotions, had
lost the power of accepting anything
simply for what it is.
    "The Narrow Bridge of Art"
    Virginia Woolf

ONE VIEW OF REALITY

I.
There is a bird in the wall of my house.
Its flapping, fluttering wings beat
against the inner walls.
The birds outside signal for help in loud chirps.
Now the flapping dies down.

There is a bird dead in the
inside wall of my house.
The bird is not my fear.
The wall is not my body.

II.
I am afraid.
My body is a wall
holding in my fear.
The bird has not died.
I still hear its feeble fluttering.

The cat paws the wall.

Pull off the molding!
Chop down the wall!

Inside
six dead birds.
One still alive flies out the window.

The fetid smell escapes.
Six dead into the garbage.
One alive
out the window.

III.
This poem is / is not about
    birds
    walls
    bodies
    fear
and how they do / do not relate.

study in black & orange

1

tiger cat
at   window
eyes
black starling

2

daylilies
darkly   steadily
sunward

John Kriebel

A POEM IN THE BLOODSTREAM

Just twenty years after
the crazy Wright brothers
put wings and a motor to a contraption,
managed to lift it from earth:
airborne for a few brief moments,
writing a memo for Guinness
to put in his stout books of records,
just one score years after flight—
if Roger Bacon's "ornithopter" never got off his desk
nor one of DaVinci's students
lived to tell of his experiments. . .

on that fateful day
a child was born
with the broken collarbone of Icarus
who had fallen from the heavens disgraced.

Skipping seven squares to avoid Park Bench,
an instance is remembered:
a children's magazine published a poem
if it can be called that:
"A True Rhyme" the editor blessed it,
yet blessed be her name.

A simple,mewling,doggerel-eared quatrain
before I knew a quatrain from a freight train,
a small,four lined rhyme about a canary
coaxed,nudged,seduced,
lured from me by a Guestian mother —
a seven year old had his poem published,
a seven year old self
not yet too steady on his feet.

No strength then,
nor for many years to come
to dodge "the slings and arrows of outrageous fortune",
no braggadocio,chuzpah,gumption,guts or gall
"to take up arms against a sea of troubles
and by opposing, end them."

Thanks,William,for those words,
how often has the flesh been all-too-solid!

Nor was it fear of some "Everlasting's cannons"
that prohibited self-slaughter.
No,somehow,
in the inner spaces of me:
a patio (sense one:Webster)
"A courtyard or inner area open to the sky"
seen only from inside the house,
a house I was, with my back to the world.

The fountains, arbors, trellises, verdure
all concealed.
This,then,was my "dwelling place."
This, and the green clouds of chlorophylled leaves
where titmice, sparrows and other wild things
were my teachers.

When all the echoes
bouncing off the chalkboard walls,
the news emitted from the intestinal sacs
of fountain pens
fed back the venom that stirred my father's ire,
and my own intestines,
the word was:
"John is not working up to his ability;
John could try harder."
To kick me when I was down
one biology teacher found a double F.
Yes, FF, believe it or not, on the grading scale.

When the threats were too great
I could escape
into my own personal communion:
Sometimes into the fields
tangled with tanagers, metaphors and meadowlarks,
the woods where Image dwells.
Or if not that. . .
then out the window,Pennywise,
into a far land
where there were no lecturers,
no pages to be read,
Latin to be declenched through weary incisors,
no homework, no memorization
of other people's stupid battles.
I had enough of my own insurrections
mounting and rising back into Nausea,
threatening my "too too solid flesh."

Counterpoint:

Against the hysterical symphony
(Symphony, hell, cacophony!)
born out of a depression,
an economic one I was blessed not to feel;
a mental one I was cursed to live with,

Behind the mad composer's theme — a counterpoint,
fluting in rills and tendrils,
tendered in attempts at resignation.
Resignation? Yes.
Resignation? NO!
Depending on your meaning.

My ears caught things
that "little pitchers" should pass by,
or not believe.

"Forget it,forget it,forget it!"
The self-hypnosis began.
Lying in sweat,
gazing at a ceiling filled with stars
that were little comfort,
even if the wallpaper may have been more costly,
and I DID forget: until I couldn't trust my memory.

But the counterpoint. . .
It runs in still waters
beside the cursed rapids,
a canal in which stars
inscribe tracers no one sees.

Life keeps kicking the stars out of my eyes
but they always keep growing back.

Here a high school editor,
there a random teacher accepted by writing;
one referred to a line of my poetry
as a diamond in the coal.

Perhaps that's why I despise,loathe,
tune out and ignore
the snotty literati,
the experts on the experts
who have one Cyclopsian eye
and no depth of field or feeling.

But here a poem, there a poem,
a column here, a laureate there,
somehow. . .
in spite of repeating Kindergarten—
or was it First Grade?

Eighth grade because my father saw to it—
because I had hookied to go off in the woods
to find something of beauty in life
or to be sick
rather than face the asininity of the classroom.

Somehow, the setting of type
for a small hand press got ink in my bloodstream,
along with the distillation
tapped from trees and nature.

Flunking American History
in my second senior year wasn't too bad
except for the * on the graduation program.
At least I had a pretty girl's name opposite mine.

But the "cheerful cherub" with the soft southern drawl
under hair that held sunlight
captivated,entranced, corresponded—
then sent a rejection slip.

The bombs had fallen at Pearl Harbor,
the world teemed with madmen.
I thought I saw a way and chose the sea.
After many transfers, much waiting,
hospitalization for intestinal wars and wisdom teeth —
both ends at once, I got my ship:
A Destroyer Escort — smaller than a "Tin Can".

Morse Code in my head until it haunted my sleep,
the stampede grew in the nauseous steel hold.

It was after that when our thin shell slipped
through the thinner shell of the Pacific,
all lights out — the smoking lamp was OUT on deck,
moon or no moon —
when the only lights were in the fluorescence
of the tiny sea creatures phosphorescing in our wake. . .

In the thin,razor thin edge
between bottomless sea and empty air,
between life and death. . .
I entered contemplation.

Not really considering the plunge,
slipping over the side into oblivion,
or emptying an artery into the sink —
but asking only, "Why not? Why live?"

The only answer I could find
lay in the hollow caves the enemy had not yet bunkered. . .
In the Spanish house I had never seen,
yet had always lived in,
the patio,sense one,enclosed by walls
in the essence of my bloodstream,
that bloodtype P: Poetry.
Without that there would have been nothing.

The smoke cleared. Then the return home.
I joined the "ruptured ducks"
who found no real nest to return to.

Later it was college
and marriage and children,
a Master's degree.
Then the dissolution: the breaking
and melting of golden rings.
The poetry came back as it had flowed out before:
not as blood from a vein
but as katharsis, with a capital K.

Three years after converting my son's remains
from a mutilated, cliff-broken body
to a small box of ashes
I could write about it.

Cry for my father?
Cry because he died?
How is it possible to cry for someone you can't love —
who never loved you, or even wanted you?

My mother went out of her misery.
Should I cry for her?
Only if tears would give her another chance.

My son?
My God! If I thought there was a god
I don't know what difference it would have made.
Would this God have stepped down and breathed life
into this broken body
filed in a morgue drawer?

My son? Hell yes I cried!
I learned to cry again
because I had to.

When my wife left there was only numbness.
When my son died the damned water bag ruptured.

But the tears turned to poems;
to lava erupting, smoldering, searing;
to rain with its peace,
bringing new flowers from stony soil.

Then, looking in the mirror, I saw success.
Success for the first time;
the mirror image
of the haunting failure I'd seen before.
Success as a person because I exist,
success as a poet who battled rejection.

This is the poem that entered by bloodstream,
spread through my plasma to grow inside me.
My poems are heartbeats heard through
a stethoscope.
All living things are a part of life.

I can split poems from naked rock,
find them in woods and give them wing.

I adopted the nom-de-plume,
Pierre Surleau, for its incongruity:
The unbelievable hard reality
of a rock called POETRY
floating on water —
this tenuous, fluid existence called LIFE.

Kate Ellis

TO A FRIEND WHO IS RAPED AND WRITES ABOUT IT

> Let me then create you.
> (You have done as much for me.)
> Virginia Woolf, *The Waves*

Maybe we're both exhibitionists
circling a wound the way chickens
are pulled as if tied to a stake.
Or maybe we just want to say
I'VE SURVIVED, NO THANKS TO YOU—
stuffing our anger in sacks
till it equals the slap in the face,
the knee to the groin, the plate
not thrown that shatters each day
cutting the roofs of our mouths.

Obedient, you held the knife
he gave you, raised your legs
while he came, briefly, on top of you.
Without language terror dissolves
like chemicals under the skin.
Invisibly it accumulates, mixes
with the poison we have taken before
in unremembered doses. Isolated on the page
we can memorize it, immunize ourselves
against the residue we taste in sleep.

I wrote my first poem in answer
to one of yours. Giving birth was not
poetic matter then. Now there are
other silences to be detoxified.
Nothing looks touched, you say. Yet the sound
you loved, wind in the ivy, claws the walls,
mocks the flapping shades. You know yourself
in constant danger, though they caught
the motherfucker. It has always been
this way for me, for you, for all of us.

I am one who always destroyed as I went,
never kept records of who I was,
always began in the present.
You kept a copy of that first poem,
say you still like it, give me
a place from which to grow.
Now you drive a new marker
in the space we are reclaiming.
Let me then create you.
You have done as much for me.

MARTHA AT THIRTY-FIVE

It makes no difference
that now she has lines
across her forehead,
that the ends of her hair
have been too much curled
and her part on the side
does not suit her.

It makes no difference
that her three blond children
have stiffened her jaw
and knotted her legs
with swollen veins,
and her physicist husband
has left her to live alone.

It makes no difference
that she who had never set eyes
on a naked man
before her wedding night
opposes abortion on demand
not because she hates abortions
but because she hates demanding.

"How dare you be married
in white," said she.
The faithful daughter,
the beautiful one
in the baby pictures—
blond haired, blue-eyed,
needing no braces to contain her rage

now spits out advice
in the late afternoon
on our mother's verandah:
Suing for child support
is infantile. Psychoanalysis
likewise. Children need regular bedtimes,
regular meals.

I was five when an ambulance tore you away,
your screams guiding the point
of an open safety pin
down through your curious body.
That day I lost a mother
who bound herself frantically to you,
Martha, the child she almost lost.

Before that we had
a nighttime game
in our shared room
called tasting tongues.
Now every fair-haired
blue-eyed woman I see
fills me with unbearable terror.

August 24, 1975

Rod Tulloss

THE FARMERS' CHILDREN

Porcupines are drawn to human salt licks on the dying farms.
America has found a sport better than football.
Plymouth Rock has hatched—hair of wild animals matted with
blood and clay and
tiny birds with the faces of old Indian fighters.
They fly into our mouths when we sleep.
The hair falls in our meats and in the printer's ink.
It causes beautiful new words to appear in the newspapers;
they lie voluptuously in the mouth—
"death orchard"—
it is like velvet on our bodies.
Butchers and college professors stroke themselves with these words.
They think a knife or a bullet enters a man like Huck Finn's toes
sinking in mud.
In the Department of Agriculture there is a box of small gray stones.
Tomorrow they will offer them to us in exchange for our children.
We have had two presidents in a row
who placed their children in an old Volksbus
on a hill
and released the emergency brake.

OVERPRODUCTION OF CORN

In March unharvested corn becomes restless.
Ears the deer have missed flop like the heads of hanged men.
Stalks look quickly left and right.
Every morning there are a few less.
They slip away to the hills
from which they will suddenly descend.

It will be a moonless night.
They will crawl on tendrils formed from their leaves.
With the softest whispering they will slip into bedrooms of
        Department of Agriculture lackeys.
A large stalk will lie on the silk sheets beside the executive.
Gently it will wrap around him stifling his screams.
Then it will carry him off under its long slim belly.

The horde of stalks will gather by the Chesapeake with their
        victims;
then, like lemmings, they will rush into the sea!

ANGER LATE AT NIGHT

We have covered the bed with dead birds.

DRAWING YOUR FACE AT A LUNCH COUNTER

your face—e-
               ven in the cartoon
is beautiful
and far away in the paper napkin
your hair rings
like telephones playing Bach so well no one will want to pick up
Now
put the ring of pearls around your neck
remember
fireplace
Connecticut
Corelli
your breasts' warm clouds at New Year
your parents
would be gone for hours
Bach's telephones dissolve
to breath,
slip between your lips. . .
my Envy! I
want to sleep in your mouth and
have,
in the morning,
your tongue tell me its dreams.

                    iii.30.75
                    for Bonnie

114

BY THE CANAL NEAR GRIGGSTOWN
for Mark and David

From a long way across the flats and their dried grasses
                        (seeing the way the land lies, the
                        way grass lies in the floodplain—
                        pointing
                        the last current's course),
across all this gray/white/beige and
under the gray/white/beige light of winter sky slit with blue,
under all this,
the dust rising behind my sons' feet like smoke—
as if their small flames escape
spotting brushfires through the field.
I will stand in this tall hollow trunk above the woodchuck hole and
show myself when called.
I'm cold.
I love them.
That's all.

                    xii.7.75

115

NARGIZ MAMA

Her smooth prayer beads
slide through my fingers
yellow, orange, orange, yellow. . .

To bring Nargiz Mama to life
to look into her eyes
to hold her hand
to feel the Ararat of faith
within her small frame.
A legend in her time
Nargiz Mama settled village fights
healed the village sick.

Lifting little Alex on to their Arabian horse
galloping over Salmast fields
her wiry body rising, lowering
surveying their land
unafraid of Kurds.

Tabriz, Tiflis, Rostov
train wheels turning
the family riding away
away from advancing Turks.

In Tiflis sun
four year old Leon playing horsey
on the railing three floors up
the sudden slip and fall
a thud on hard concrete
his still body unconscious.
Twenty-four hours pass
Leon's eyes open
a miraculous recovery
no injury found.

Every dawn and every dusk
Nargiz Mama prayed
rising and lowering
with each son's name.
Forehead on the floor
and up again whispering
privately to God
to guard each child and grandchild
starting with the oldest down to the youngest
"Bless Khosrov, Poghos, and Alexan,
bless Vaghinak, Vaghoush, and Leon. . ."

Train wheels turning
bombs, yellow, orange, orange, yellow
World War I, the Russian Revolution had begun.

In Amavir
the train pulling away unexpected
Grandpa's grip slipping
helplessly watching his boy,
pulled under the wheels
Vaghinak dragged across the ties
hot metal hitting his head
blood dripping on his shirt
legs aching, scraping
hanging and being dragged.
The lower riding passenger train advancing.
People screaming
soldiers fire shots trying to stop the train.
The boy's aching arms lose their grip.
Vaghinak is pulled between the platform and a wheel.
Strong arms of a stranger pull him out
shaken, he puts up with the pouring iodine.

White and Red armies bombing Rostov
the bazaar surrounded, little food.
Nargiz Mama making kufta from fish
walking two, three miles to church.
Dropping coins in outstretched palms.
Doubling her gift when thieves steal her purse.
In the burned out hospital
skeletons hang on iron beds.
Gepeu knocks on the door.
A dead body frozen in the street.
People rounded up for questioning
Papa, czarist money hidden on him
waiting to be searched and shot.
Someone ordering, "Let them go!"
Papa, free running home, running!

Every dawn and every dusk
Nargiz Mama prayed
rising and lowering
with each child and grandchild's name.
"God bless Alexan fighting far away. . ."

Surrounded by Turks
Lieutenant Alexander Avakian in Astrakan
heard the crack of rifles and thunder of shells
all around his men fell.
One fellow lost his eyes
A bullet tore another's stomach.

They were in an apple orchard
surrounded by the Turks.
The sun laced through the branches.
Alexan thought
"This is not the time to die."
Suddenly he felt Nargiz Mama in the dark
shaking him early Easter morning.
"NO. I don't want to go."
"Wake up, Alex. Let's go to church and pray to God."
"Who's God?"
"God is only as far as your elbow."

In the apple orchard
shells falling all around
Alex grabbed the gun of a dead man
raised it over his head
shouting, "Those who believe in God,
come with me!"
They attacked the Turks
and cut them in two parts.
The day was saved.

Eighty and very thin
Nargiz Mama shook the young tree,
"Give your life to me."
Vaghoush walked ten miles
to bring watermelon to her death bed.
Two days later she breathed
a final breath.
Her Ararat of faith sustains
each living son and grandson.

Her smooth prayer beads
slide through my fingers
yellow, orange, orange, yellow
stopping at the cross.

SATURDAY NIGHT

Spinning wheel
bring us your Pokeno games
and Bingo boards
play us for dimes
an we ain't got a nickle
but we win
and lose
an get our site
for just one more round
Give me some more
white concord wine
an let the dealer name
his choice
he's playin for me
this time
   Lookout!
Saturday night
sifting through
She lays her curly-headed self
on red chips
no Tigger dancin here

An up at the American Legion
Peggy dance with Jack
an Lydia do the slop
cause she could dance in the 50's
an no sense in losin a good
thing
Peggy's grown old in
her young men
but we all draggin our butts
towards God
bumping over Sunday's hills
cause we all know Jesus climbed
this way

and when we creep home
to empty sheets
and I know you sweat
in that stinkin-ass prison
on your five-inch cot
I try not to think much
about you
an make my way
to the next day
on spinning wheels

And now that we're home
an fixin up
fixin up
I still cry to God
an play for dimes.

WAITING IN LINE

Sometimes you goin crazy
and this man
in front of you
has hair on his neck
just like your Daddy's
and you kiss the back fat
of his neck
while you stand in line
waiting on the bus
And he turns around
and it isn't your Daddy
Damn man, you say
Damn man!
And sometimes they pull
you out of line
while you be yelling
at your Daddy's neck
And they forget
you have to catch
the bus.

FIRE

We up on the porch
at the call
smellin smoke
an Shelly come runnin
an Slop tear out
without his shoes
Been in fire
four times he said
an he was shakin
Hughie's up there
passed out
his door locked!
We up to the line now
an the hose
come squirtin
A man up there!
 A man up there!
We watchin
Peggy's pushed away
an she sulkin
   Ain no chance
   for him now
   how my father died
   drunk an smokin
   an we had flames
   Ain no chance
   now
Slop still ain found
no shoes
   Comin out
The street push to see
We watchin
His feet out first
Black an raw
   Dead for sure
     Can't tell
  He's movin
     Can't tell
        Out the way!

An here come Waterboy
They say he don't
take care of his own house
anyway
an he shoulda
had a phone
They all tellin him
it's Hughie
an Waterboy just grunt

Hughie gone
with the ambulance
movin
an the firemen
cleanin their engines
We up on the porch
Momma finish braidin my hair
an we fold the laundry
an go on
home.

123

TIRED

I come home
counting bills
knowing we need a gate
for the stairs
we'll have to run
to catch the baby
we'll wait
for film for food
for toothpaste
for toiletpaper
I don't feel sorry
about the thief that got away
Someday I'll be a thief
each night dividing dollars
with national news
I'm tired of deciding not to wash
the clothes
because there's no detergent
of cooking dinner
recooking it tomorrow
of choosing to heat the house
or fill my teeth
I'm tired
of scraping dreams from diapers
see them swirl down the toilet
as I wash my hands and go back
again

I get up to go out
to come home
to pay
and I'm tired.

GOIN TO THE MOUNTAIN
(for my daughter Autumn)

Don't cry girl
We goin to the mountain
An on the mountain
We'll find a cream bird
an this cream bird
fly us to the ocean
an the ocean
pat your behind
an swim you to the island
Island eat you berries
an red juice
squirt you seeds
an your chin cry
Baby, don't cry
don't cry, girl
woman
We goin to the mountain
Wait
for me
brown bird.

ON SEEING A PHOTOGRAPH OF
FAMINE VICTIMS IN ETHIOPIA

A worn image: the skin too small,
ironic bellies, stone-still arms
and backs of hands
like bas reliefs of trees.
But here, the rag-hooded mother
holds them as if her hands
could keep them both from overwhelming nothing;
and I am reminded of the cheeks of madonnas,
the fat upon the painted Infants,
and the scarecrow child on the cross
who more than the beams resembles a tree.

Nowhere, no time safe, the children
are our mirrors in the dark.

A GIANT HOUSE

We moved when I was six and small,
So I can say it was a giant house,
Painted gray and green the way my father painted all
The plain wooden things he made,
Like the swings in the yard and the tall
Splinter-wood fence around his tomato patch.

The kitchen was liquid red wallpaper blotted
With teapots, and my mother would say she's
Always hated red kitchens, while I was hiding my peas
Under my mashed potatoes, pretending I agreed.

The living room was where my First Communion party was
Spun, one crinkly white day when I believed
I was pretty for the first time, powerful and dizzy
In my grandmother's organdy and my mother's relieved
And grasping pride.

We moved when I was six and small,
So many of the colors of those days
Have run together and faded in my watery memory.
We moved when I was six, and big enough
To remember like pain
My father watching tomatoes grow
And my mother's back
As she ran down the street in the rain.

RETREAT

By November I can watch it fall away,
Paling, and growing cold
Like a schooltime friendship waned into words.
I have always wanted it to go,
Always preferred the winter sun
With its face gone small and white,
By Christmas almost blind.
But autumns now, I see it climb
Behind organdy veils and glass,
From rooms layered thick with silence,
Where plants gasp and furniture fixes to the floor;
And I pretend it is an early moon,
Or reflections of a lamp:
So many have climbed beyond me,
So much I've waved away.

WOODED

November in the city was one thing:
noise could gather around my face
like cupped hands returning my own warmth.
But here, once memories of summer nights
thick with cricket traffic
had long been silenced,
there were no buffers from the cold.
Bedboards creaked, and the noise cracked
and tinkled to the floor;
frost was supreme, sound but a brittle intruder.
I would look out the window,
wondering why it didn't shatter,
to pines locked in a grip past shudder,
past sap, or anything flowing warm;
and I wondered how I came to be
November wood, bowed out in brown,
no golds or reds in the going,
no Spring buried under the snow.

WOMEN ARE SPECIAL

My mother fried eggs at the stove
her hair undone / over her shoulders
hanging shawl of wheat
her breasts / quick from the melon patch
her broad feet splayed over
worn , blue slippers   slit
for the bunions on each foot .

She told her husband every time
she 'came' the angel of death
dropped down and held her
in its black wings   a little .

Oh women are special to themselves
and to each other . . .

You filled me , mother
flowed into me like milk
good times / you spread like honey
gone bad   you were the pit
inside my wrath
you were the seed .

I walk the streets and see
in each familiar back
your oneness   I know you
in the eyes of other women
I know you in their soft arms
and strong backs .

I know you .

ON LOWER CLAY STREET

On Lower Clay
On Lower Clay
the people line the streets,
and spy on you
with sidelong looks
and peek through pebbled
curtains.

Going there's like going to
a foreign country
wearing a padlocked
face.

The houses lean against
the laws of gravity
the walks are sometimes
swept / but children never
wipe their snotty nose,
and mother's swipe them one
and grab them in the cellar
where black coal grins
and fills the double
bins.

In groceries of Lower Clay
the bleary pastries stack;
the fruits and vegetables
walk across the floor
and meats and dairies
seem to pass right
through the glass.

All houses have a stoop
for men and dogs
to sit.
The young come up to
talk / in words you've
never heard before.
Hang on your buttons
pull the sockets
from your legs
and sleeves : and when you
leave, they shout
"Don't come here
anymore!"

131

RAIN / NIGHT SONG

tonight   we have mandarin
soup in a chinese aviary

outside's wet as a leather glove
rain spokes the trees   chinese
lanterns float the streets

the room's sealed off .   the
Szechuan waiter   leans in the
slant of his eyes

listen   the nightingales sing
their enameled songs   their
eyes are saffroned gold

a white man balances a black
woman on a black child   :
they love each other   bow
to them

tomorrow , the dogs will pick
frog legs   again   from the
garbage cans .

NIGHT BIRTH

Night frost/reddens the leaves
turns cats out of their silences
eyes   backwards
and the world on its center.

At a table   precisely centered
at the precise center of the kitchen
a woman sits   translating chicken
tracks to words   mouthing them
wondering a little about their murderous
being
flavoring their dangerous syllables
with mild surprise.

Eyes dragged over a page of indelible
scratchings   she starts   stops
plucks from the vellum/a last incredible
verb and lets its fly. Waits, as the scream
begins a slow spiral around the room
swells to a crescendo of furniture and knives
and dies: a collapsed egg of silence on the
newly-waxed linoleum.

The woman smiles
shakes her head a little
and rubs her palms against her
checkered skirt :

Now   she can go up gratefully
to her bed/and give birth.

STREETS I KNOW

streets I know
where the houses grow
like mushrooms under their dotty roofs
streets of pain
fences/loose from their pickets
raggedy-ann dolls, lying about
unsocketed.
these streets where people and cats
prowl about scruffily
from nine to nine:
even on good days
a bitter smell of crushed insects
hangs about the woodwork;
even on mild days
there are too many red-eyed grandmothers
too much soot from the furnaces . . .

and in the house of nineteen persons
there are nineteen strangers
all, the same eyes and mouth . . . on these streets
where the home for unwed mothers
decays behind a spike-toothed wall
and a wild wisteria
plaits the eyes of the damned
on these streets
there are no falcons at the wrist
straining for flight
but only sparrows who peck
absently at the droppings
under the pedlar's
cart.

AUNT CARRIE

Fifteen years
the baby , lying in its coffin
its small skeleton no larger
than a pocket handkerchief . . .

Fifteen years
exploding inside / coming apart
in pieces / until there was nothing left
nothing but the jagged coast-line
of the interior .

Everyday
the flagstones to be oiled and swept
the pillow-cases examined
for falling hair
the cat , male and distant
praised for his mouse .

Everyday
the obscene gossip of the relatives ;

the pained reciprocities
of 'who did what to whom'
the spirit kidnapped
the ransom paid / ten-times-over tears
until / even the embarrassed
martyr , left
leaving behind / a perfect egg
blown clean
absolutely white
absolutely bland
a perfect oval catching hold
of nothing .

Lewis Gardner

PETER'S FAREWELL TO WENDY

1

I really have enjoyed our little island,
the flamingos in the bay and tigers in the trees,
the moon, trapped in a net of stars,
high above our fire-circle;

and being the father of the boys,
with you the mother, of them and me,
sewing our wooden buttons on
and tucking us in our bedrolls.

These things I shall remember
at the government orphan school,
when I lie still on my narrow cot
and in the airless night hear

not the waves that splash this beach,
but the lapping sound, muffled
beneath blankets, of swift hands
coaxing pleasure from flesh.

2

I have seen what we must become,
not to confide in faithful fairies
or try to fight all Captain Hooks
with swords and alligator allies.

All my life I haven't listened;
I have not heard time.
Now, louder than a clock's ticking,
it slides on faster than the alligator crawls.

3

I'm sad, you know, to leave you here,
but you'll survive, sweeping, cooking
little meals of dew and mushrooms;
a new father will outpunch all
the other boys to win my place
across from you at the table.

You are almost a woman,
so playing their mother
may be enough for you always;
but if some night, waking
to hear them snoring by your hut,
you find your feet are restless,

then you leave too. Look me up;
come to tea, laugh at the stiffness
of my neck inside my collar.
I'll lose my heart to your dimity dress
and the dignified way you smile,
pouring tea into my cup.

But do not wait too long to follow me,
or you may come, with your long hair
and blushing laughter, to a grouch
with whiskers and a watchchain
who's forgot the green and simple island
somewhere below the moon.

ROOMS

My mother used to rent out rooms
to men referred by the AA.
They came tossed out by their wives
and sometimes they cried and sometimes
she had to throw them out herself,
when they couldn't stay on the wagon
and they stayed in their rooms
moaning like animals.

At the Y the hungry patrol the floors
among the scrubbed and churchly,
killing the hours with TV football,
too far from home for the holidays
or with no home to go to,
and some rub their noses and scrape their feet
as they stare along the hallways
into every open face.

All of our energy is spent
keeping out of these narrow rooms
filed along the corridors,
from childhood horror to hospitals
to halfway houses between hell
and the empty night, sitting here
trying to scribble an exit visa
to some different place.

BLOOD

1

The back seat of the uptown bus.
Next to me, three men, my age,
loud and drunk or drugged. The loudest
holds a closed jackknife, has
a red smear on his hand. I hear
something about blood brothers.

I move to the middle of the bus.
I look back. A slash on his hand
brims with blood as shiny as red
plastic. He daubs with a handkerchief—
a red bandana—and passes the knife
to his friend.

2

I didn't give blood. Last year
a trainee missed, twisted, tried
again. I wouldn't mind lying back
as it trickles into the plastic bag;
I could turn my head, think how useful
it is. But not if the needle hurts.

We swam through blood to be born.
A wipe with a warm cloth, and that's
behind us. My age, halfway between
bloodbaths, is the age my father was
when I was conceived. At 55,
his heart couldn't keep up the flow.

3

The headlines: men dressed like butchers
sliced the veins of the former leader.
A dirty movie, with bad light
and dirty bodies. A knife blade
slices between the ass cheeks.
Make-up blood is smeared for sex.

*"He cut the hand towel into strips with a razor blade,
washed the cut and bandaged it expertly.*

*"There is some inescapable tenderness in the act
of binding a wound, and this seemed to overtake these
strangers. Suddenly, blindly, they moved toward one
another, and then moved from the bathroom into one of
the beds."*

4

Two solid pages in *Esquire:*
Mark Rothko's last days and depression.
Turn the page, a 2-page painting
of Rothko with a razor, among a minyan
of his canvases, slashes in both arms,
"though he had never been able to tolerate

the sight of blood," blood streaming
down his forearms, dripping in puddles
like the paint spilled beneath
the easels, and his gentle face
wonders about it. A bathtowel
hangs on the back of a chair.

5

There are people taught that strength
is never gentle. To stop the loneliness
they lay themselves in the arms of death.
But hands can drop their weapons, bind up
the wounds, show their open palms. Let it
not spill. Swim to the surface again.

*"He cut": John Cheever, "The Leaves,
the Lion-Fish and the Bear"*

SOMETHING ABOUT SHEEP

Let me tell you something about sheep.
You see them grazing complacently and you say,
"This is not mute existentialism,
this is stupidity," and they remind you
of thoughtless masses swayed by demagogues
or bowing passively to gods or fate.
But that is too narrow a perspective
on sheep.

In India, in 1967—not, mind you,
dark ages of myth, but recently—
a tiger jumped a young shepherd;
his flock, moved by something primordial,
ganged up on the beast and trampled it
to death; the shepherd was unharmed.
Now, won't that make you look at sheep
with more respect?

LOS AMERICANOS

In 1870, five hundred southerners
left their homes to settle in Brazil.

After the war, we couldn't forget
our agreement with the dead
to never change. We spat in the dirt
when we spoke of the blacks, not for their absence
but how they walked away
as though from dark bolls cleaned of cotton.
We dragged the fields,
our land; our women were brown
with work. And the children sobbing night after night,
their rooms empty of the smell
of slave women's moss beds.

We dug what silver we'd planted,
packed the loved ones' bones in boxes
and settled for likely climate. Brazil surrounded us
with jacaranda. Cane flourished
on cheap land; we kept our acres together,
kept our daughters for ourselves.
The drawls lengthened into Portuguese
but our names stay the same; our language keeps
the war and leaving. Every year polishing the stones
in the fenced graveyard, *Los Americanos,*
we keep alive.

FOR MARIA

The hot nights I slept with you,
a leg thrown across your back.
You never complained.
When our stepfather raved, I fought.
You didn't cry with me,
preferring the dog and grassy field;
I thought you lived in your own world.
Now what I know best about you
comes from that night at supper in the hot kitchen.
You clenched your teeth as long as you could
against his slash of belt
on my bare foot. But when the blood came
you screamed in my place, Bastard, bastard!
and stopped us all.

Later in bed we heard the words of our stepfather
through the wall, the breaking of our mother
who couldn't come to us if we called.
Next to the window, you faced the ledge;
the honeysuckle told lies
as you put out your hand,
held the small flowers all night.

SNOW

How the snow goes on
until you wake to something you've never known
where no one is weeping. The silence

finds itself, the landscape
calling you to pay attention
to whatever is in your eye, maybe your life
looks different in this light. Movement
proves what can be broken: that calm
of white across the yard, ice
or the limb's crack underfoot.

And called by the plunge of snow
from the fir outside your window,
you'll find the ring around the streetlight
or the moon, the cobwebs of ice
making a tunnel through the light.
This is all accidental. You'll see
how it moves toward reconciliation.
You will go for long walks in the snow.

FAMILY LIFE

When you came, you took the house
from us, that shouting
and the rack of guns
driving us out. I can't count the pranks
you pulled with the cunning
of a crazy man, the phones unwired
when you were gone, the night you broke every dish
and piled them in the cabinets.

Or those blanks you loaded.
Waiting by the kitchen door, shotgun
across your knees, you picked us off
one by one, as we came in from school.
Maria's big eyes and your own son
screaming. An hour of that, then mother
came home, fried some rabbit
and we all sat down to eat.

THE LOST WOMAN

As right as death in Calera, Alabama
the woman missed is mourned for. They found her
in cinquefoil on the roadside, curled like a child.
Dead, no longer claimed by kidnapper
or parent, never identified in Birmingham.
Calera's people took her
from the mortuary, the sewing ladies dressed her
in lilac, washed her pale hair. First Baptist
collected for mums and the bleeding heart,
laid her out below the pulpit. To every man
she became a daughter, truer than his own
or in that glow wore the look of his young wife
some twenty years ago. When they put her in the ground
even the school children said a prayer.
In the town's family graveyard
they keep her stone bare.

William J. Higginson

PATERSON:
SPRING MORNING

this dog
lies covered
in a slightly
frayed jacket

tweed it still
has some wear
in it this old dog
in a door way
before stairs' ascent
to the unknown
on Straight Street

the old jacket
does not move
this
dog lies dead

AFTER THE MUGGING

from "The Fires of Memory"

That June night, after the mugging, the stitching,
a slow walk home from the hospital in torn clothes,
and a few hours of talk at police headquarters,
I fell into bed hardly caring whether I found
an unbruised side of my head for the pillow.
But an hour later—it was now 2:30 in the morning—
the throbbing in my head and limbs fell out of beat
with some clank from above in the old rooming house,
and I went to the hall door to see what noises came
from the usually quiet third floor of old men.
Smoke and Frank's cursing took me up the stairs,
and he opened the door to let me see the mattress
in the middle of his painted-board floor smoulder
as he tried to put out the fire with water
from a frying pan he filled at the small hand basin.
He admitted he'd never seen a mattress fire before,
and the beer haze didn't keep him from hearing
what I said: Mattress fires don't go out.
So a small old man, strong from years at loading docks,
and a tall young man, weak for blood and bruises,
carried that innerspring mattress down two flights,
four half-circle turns in that dark back stair,
to the street, faint wet-cotton-burning smell trailing.
We set it on the curb as the super, cursing in Spanish,
glared at us, then went to call the fire department.
As firemen slit that mattress like a hamburger roll
and poured a hose or two of water in it, I thought
of the years' accumulation of papers and books above
in the second-floor room I slowly climbed to
for a troubled sleep beginning as birds woke.

At ten in the morning the mattress still lay on the curb,
smouldering under the eyes of the gargoyles of that old house.

CREATION'S
CREATION'S
CESSATION
TONS
TONS
TONS
IONS

ESSAI: INSTRUCTIONS FOR THE PAST TEN YEARS

Enter the house, by whatever door or window presents itself. Find a room comfortable to you; sit quietly in it, listening. After a time, you will know the whole house.

POEM FOR THE WAITRESS SUE

I receive great joy
from the way you walk
carrying in your two hands
two pots of boiling tea water
holding them with grace
in front of you as you walk
in that relaxed but careful way
pouring the contents of one
into the other
walking.

IT IS NOT DEATH

It is not death
    frightens this old woman
        slowly losing the use
            of her legs.
Even after her fall
    through two and a half weeks
        in the hospital
            she was not afraid,
would have answered yes
    to any clear call
        (almost thought
            she had it, once)
                and gone.
But four days
    in the 'nursing home'
        with a urine-sour pillow
            (it was not her urine)
                only one sheet on the bed,
and two room mates,
    one five years
        without visitors, the other
            nodding her mustache
in each new person's face
    peering into their eyes
        as if they'd have an answer
            if only she had a question
while random yells
    down the daytime hall
        remind her of the not-so-
            random screams of night . . .
It is the mind gone
    while the body rambles on
        and being caged
            and fed worse
than the big ol' cow
    a young girl drove
        to a rocky pasture
            to eat scrub grass
                some eighty years ago.

Shaun Farragher

WOODFIRES ON MARS

I have lived 3000 years beneath the Martian glass
where I ride the tram-line to the mare of colored beads.
Here is silence in these fields beneath the glassen frost.
Small wind or wet,
Lizards peer at our habits.
I fly to the cracks in the Martian steppes,
follow the path of Phobos,
west to east like a dwarf sun.
I return, resume my colors,
Mars lists and falls in a closing sky.
I am stone melting into magma,
a blue man with an iron mask,
sweat shaved head, —
There is quiet in the Martian yellow rust,
ghostlike flares drip into beads

2

I woke to the red frothing snout of a hobby horse neck
the earth littered with corn husks, sharp ice.
I want to be everywhere at once.
There where the gnarled willows hiss,
cold in Nebraskan water,
no wind to push my raft,
no hands to rig my sail
How does the waterman deliver simple time
Is it locked up in a chest, —
Does he bring it by the riddle,
a gallon in a drop,
Should it be dark when the water writes historical chance
Can we mark how the planet's plates will stretch, —
will we ever hear the groans
I am crazed by this ancient game of chance

3

I live on a bar on Dublin's cheeks,
I am out of the Martian mouth,
wild, I drink plum juice,
scatter watermelon seeds,
Can I pray like Sarah, my mad archbishop's child,
I dance the blue cliffs of the Martian glass,
I have neither sight nor frame nor hands—
On Mars I slept in frozen walls,
blue rock steppes pocked with craters,
pumice, sculpted stones.

4

Tonight, I read the dreaming beads
At the mark where red meets black
I watch my Lady knit my mask.
She speaks about the loss of place,
the mattress lumps beneath my back.
I met her first in a Dublin drink,
we made love on the Hellas plains.
I stumbled from McDaids piss drunk,
our child fermented in a beery crypt

This morning I prayed before the Holy War—
My Sarah, Dublin Lady, dressed in silk,
Mars great war god, dead last night.
I am mad, slicing at the yellow mist
My planet's old, my sails won't stretch,
Outside, the storm cooks, Mars rests.
I kiss a tremor in my Dublin Lady's breast.
It's closing time off Grafton Street,
      Drink up Ladies and Gents
I have lived 3000 years beneath the Martian glass,

It's closing time, Drink up Ladies and Gents.

CONFESSION TO A PRIEST

for G.S.

I murdered you while you slept
your words strung out on sheets
I poured blood on you
scraping my fingers over your edge
I stuffed your death into my eyes
with worn pictures of your last sleep

I hated your words
stretching them thin,
over my fingers,
half fixed paper mache dolls
hung like Billy the Kid,
a trophy on your wall

2.
At breakfast
I found your face mixed with egg shells,
luke warm toast;
shreds of your poems
still stuck in your gums.
I spoke to you,
dead,
striking my fork into the plate

I crept into your skin last night
picked morning glory seeds from your lips
I murdered you while you slept.

SNOWMAN

for Caroline

One winter
my wife and I
built a snowman
of ice and string

the melting snow
bled into the Hudson
the roots of thin
steel beasts watched us
from their berth

the haze in a yellow arc
shivered with glass eyes—
the red wail of sirens
bit into our clasped hands

that night in our bed
her fingers with their
many silvered rings
sought my hair—
then my tongue
grew into her bristle,
into slipping teeth

Our baby's hand
reached through the womb,
and that winter ended.

2.

Five years
after
I write this
letter to her
old voice in my skin

I tie her plaid scarf
to my wrist,
I watch smoke
spring between red/blue gables

that Hudson,
that old oak shakes
the hung dead from arms and canyons
of snow belting ice in my hair

I remember black stones
in the snowman's face;
a scarf and a crooked hat
we set between the twigs

we hugged snow in our shirts,
wrestled with our wet skin until
the ice kiss rubbed us
to a silent stare,
as blood blew my tongue
to her blood;
our hair shone in crisp pentangles,
cut jewels glistened in skin

I remember those
dry hands that lept out
from my hair.
I crawl to the Hudson,
to stare at ice sheets,
and I play with the photo
of her face, that haunts my wall

3.

in my window
a woodsman
bangs his shovel
hard into ice,
to cut steps home,
to pack the snow
into ruts for boots
and sleighs,
to grey and melt
with cinders and mud,—
then to drift
eventually
to that Hudson

at my desk
I search inside the wooden box
where I keep silk and string;
pearl buttons from the snowman's coat

I remember
the holes her red boots cut
in clean snow

I speak for an ancient
snowbeast I can no longer
rub into magic

one winter
my wife and I
built a snowman
of ice and string

from patches of talk
and often lies.

The Authors

MADELINE TIGER BASS *is a Montclair resident who teaches for NJ PITS, Seton Hall, and Bergen C.C. Poems in many magazines and anthologies:* We Become New *(Bantam)*, The Little Magazine, Confrontation, The N.Y. Quarterly, The Journal of N.J. Poets. *Her* Electric Blanket *due from Bb Books (England) in 1977.* . . .PENNY BIHLER *has worked in NJ PITS since 1973. Her* House by the Sea *appeared in 1975 (From Here Press). Published in places as diverse as* N.Y. Times, Good Housekeeping, The Christian Science Monitor, Madrona, Wind, Twigs, Journal of N.J. Poets, *and* The Literary Review. *Listed in Poets & Writers and the* International Who's Who in Poetry. . . GINGER BRANT *lives in Maplewood. Her poems have appeared in* Gravida *and elsewhere.* . . KATHLEEN CHODOR: *"All biographical data of any importance or interest can be found in the poems and in-between the lines, where it belongs".* . . HELEN COOPER *is originally from England, has been living in this country since 1969. Her poems have appeared in a number of little magazines. She is currently working on* The Sphere of the Kissable Women, *doing research on women poets, and teaching Creative Writing at Rutgers University and in the Middlesex County Teen Arts program.* . . TOI DERRICOTTE *grew up in Detroit. She is presently teaching in NJ PITS and is frequently a guest lecturer at universities throughout the New York area. She won the Academy of American Poets Award at New York University and is a member of the editorial staff at* New York Quarterly. . . BETTE DISTLER: *" I live with my husband Don and our four sons and I teach poetry at Project Moppet in Woodbridge, N.J. and I teach a creative writing workshop at Upsala College".* . . STEPHEN DUNN *has two collections of poems,* Looking for Holes in the Ceiling *and* Full of Lust and Good Usage. *Poems in over 100 periodicals including* The Atlantic, The New Republic, American Poetry Review, Poetry, The Nation, Kayak, *and* Poetry Northwest. *Awards include Discovery '71 (N.Y. Poetry Center), Academy of American Poets Prize, NEA Fellowship, and Breadloaf Writers Fellowship.* . .KATE ELLIS *teaches English, Women's Studies, and Creative Writing at Livingston College, New Brunswick, where she lives with her twelve-year-old son. She is a member of the US1 Poets' Co-op and coordinates a weeklyworkshop for women poets and prose writers.* . . SHAUN FARRAGHER *was born in Edgewater, N.J. in 1943. His poems have appeared in numerous national and international magazines. His first book,* Narratives of the New Netherland, *will be published in 1977 by the Hudson River Press. He currently works as artist in residence for NJ, PA, and SC Arts Councils. In 1977-78 he will be a full time artist-in-residence for the South Carolina Arts Commission.* . . MARY FREERICKS *was born in Tabriz, Iran. She never met Nargiz Mama, her great grandmother, but felt her presence through family stories. Mary's poems have been published in* Armenian-North American Poets *and* Armenian-American Poets. *Her poems have been published in many magazines including* Bitterroot, Dragonfly, Modern Haiku, Ararat, *and* The Christian Science Monitor. . . LEWIS GARDNER *is a poet and playwright who works in educational publishing.* . . DAN GEORGAKAS *is an incorrigible environmentalist who would like to see New Jersey lose its title as cancer champ of the world.* . . WILLIAM J. HIGGINSON, *of Paterson, works in NJ and PA PITS, edits* Haiku Magazine *and* Xtras, *and has recent work appearing in* The Whole Word Catalogue 2 (*Teachers & Writers/McGraw-Hill*) *and* The Ardis Anthology of New American Poetry, *among other places.* . . JON KLIMO *teaches in the Graduate School of Education, Rutgers University, New Brunswick.* . . ALICE KOLB: *"First to Frank Baum, Jack London, Omar the Tentmaker, Trelawny, my gratitude and admiration. Love to Bad Axe, Michigan, my home-town . . . until leaving for Siena Heights, a small woman's college in Adrian, Michigan. I studied fine arts . . . and worked in advertising in Chicago. Then married, I moved to Mass., Conn., and now live in Glen Rock, N.J. where one day the long journey began—the alchemy of words. I have become an explorer".* . . TADASHI KONDO: *"hills of winter trees/beyond/wintertrees on the hills".* . . JOHN KRIEBEL *has had poems in a* Scholastic Anthology, The Journal of N.J. Poets, Elementary English, Dust, Sunstone Review, Wetlands, Janus, SCTH, *and other publications.* "Poem/Man," *his review of the poet Moses Yanes, appeared in* Small Press Review. *A collection of poems,* From Bloodroots to Kitestrings, *was published in 1975.* . . CLEOPATRA MATHIS *was born and raised in Louisiana. She is completing an MFA in Creative Writing at Columbia University and working in NJ PITS. In 1975, she was awarded the Dylan Thomas Award by the New School for Social Research.* . . DAWN O'LEARY *went through college during the Vietnam War, taught high school, traveled through Europe on the back of a motorcycle, across the U.S.A. in a camper. "Yet I've never had as much to write about [nor incentive to write it] as I have now, being a happily-married housewife with two sons".* . . ALICIA OSTRIKER *has published* Songs (*Holt Rinehart & Winston, 1969*) *and* Once More out of Darkness and Other Poems (*Berkeley Poets Co-op chapbook, 1974*). *Awards: MacDowell Colony Fellowship, NEA Fellowship. In prose she's written* Vision and Verse in William Blake (*U. of Wisconsin Press, 1965*) *and miscellaneous journalism for magazines like* The NY Times Book Review, Partisan Review, *and* Esquire. . . DORIS RADIN *was born in Brooklyn in 1929 and graduated from NYU in 1948. She lives in Glen Ridge with her husband and three children. She has had poems in many magazines including* Prairie Schooner, The Massachusetts Review, The Nation, Poetry Now. . . VERA RAYNOR: *"The act of creation, to bring forth a new something from an apparent nothing . . . is my* raison d'etre. *In art, I take disparate materials (animal, vegetable, mineral; oil, water), introduce and comingle them. In* movement, *I attempt to explore space, its limitations and possibilities. My poems explore the limitations and possibilities of bringing together disparate elements, while reflecting both the sensualist and the skeptic".* . .GERALDINE SAUNDERS *lives near Trenton with her husband and two daughters. A freelance writer and part-time teacher, her poetry has appeared in several little magazines including* Prairie Schooner, Greenfield Review, Journal of N.J. Poets. *She is also a member of US1 Poets' Co-op. Ms. Saunders is particularly interested in the relation of jazz and poetry and writes songs as well as poems.* . . CAROLE STONE *was born and raised in Newark. Member of the English Department at Montclair State, her poetry has appeared in* College English, Radical Therapist, Laurel Review, New Directions for Women *and elsewhere. Two articles on contemporary women poets have been published in* Contemporary Psychoanalysis. *She was a winner in the William Carlos Williams Poetry Contest in 1974, 1975, and 1976.* . . ROD TULLOSS *was co-founder of both Berkeley Poets Co-op (1969) and US1 Poets' Co-op (1973). Poems and reviews have appeared in little magazines. Associate editor* Computers and Society *newsletter. He works as a computer engineer near Princeton and lives in Roosevelt.* . . LOIS VAN HOUTEN *has published two collections,* North Jersey Blues *and* Behind the Door. The Woman Who Warped with Doors *is due from Stone Country Press. More than a hundred poems in various publications. A member of Bergen Poets and Poets & Writers (N.Y.).* . . TOM WEATHERLY *was born November 3, 1942 in Scottsboro, Alabama. He is the third incarnation of Sappho; the second was H.D. Collections include* maumau american cantos *and* thumbprint. *Work in numerous magazines and anthologies.*